A FLIGHT TO NOWHERE

Gordon Olson

authorHOUSE®

AuthorHouse™
1663 Liberty Drive, Suite 200
Bloomington, IN 47403
www.authorhouse.com
Phone: 1-800-839-8640

This book is a work of non-fiction. Unless otherwise noted, the
author and the publisher make no explicit guarantees as to the
accuracy of the information contained in this book and in some

First published by AuthorHouse 3/26/2008

ISBN: 978-1-4343-5627-7 (sc)

Printed in the United States of America
Bloomington, Indiana

This book is printed on acid-free paper.

DEDICATION

I dedicate this book to members of the crew of NR Four whom may be here no longer, and to God for without his help I would not be here.   He has inspired me to write this book a tale I felt had to be told.

PREFACE

There comes a time in a person's life when one sits down and wonders what have I accomplished, and what memorable events have happened.

Do they warrant a place in history?   Or are they forgettable in the passing parade of one's life.

I think back and I feel I have led an interesting time in my sojourn on earth, but of all the times and places I have experiences on particular segments of time fifty years ago almost to the days stands out, because the events of my life could have easily stopped there, and there were many times where this might have happened.

There were many interesting times in the first two years I in the Navy, but this story is mainly about the last two years and the dangers we faced climaxing on the day we lost our world a flight to nowhere.

CONTENTS

BIO OF THE AUTHOR

Gordon Olson was born 1933 in Hibbing, Minnesota, attending Hibbing High School and Junior College.

After spending four years in the Navy from 1952 to 1956 he attended North Dakota State University graduating with a degree in Architecture.

After spending thirty years designing buildings he retired and now lives in San Marcos, California thirty miles north of San Diego.

During his retirement he has found time to delve back into art, and is an accomplished, and award winning water colorist. He has also found time to teach art to the elderly, and also found time to write his memories down in this book.

N

WAIMIER FALS

ESCAPE & EVASION

NAHA

AIR STATION

PEARL HARBOR — FORD ISL.

AREA OF WOOM TOOMS

HONOLULU

OKINAWA SCALE 1"=10 MI.

BARBERS POINT
N. A. S.

WAIKIKI

DIAMOND HEAD

OAHU HAWAII SCALE 1"=10 MI.

TOKYO

TOKYO
BAY

MANILA

YOKOHAMA

MANILA BAY

ATSUGI N.A.S.

YOKOSUKA

SANGLEY POINT N.A.S.

KAMAKURA

CAVITI CITY

JAPAN SCALE 1" = 10 MI.

PHILIPPINES SCALE 1"=10MI.

CHAPTER 1
THE BEGINNING

"Join the Navy and see the world", that's what the recruiter said, and he was not that far from wrong. I did land on most of the rocks (that's what we called most small islands in the pacific), and I saw a lot of that part of the world, including Japan, and I could have almost died over China. My only regret was that I never got to travel to Europe in my four years in the Navy from June 9, 1952 to June 1956.

Why the Navy you may ask? Well, my best friend joined six months before me. Lenny and I met in Confirmation in 1948 where we were the only boys because of the Polio epidemic, and became the best of friends. We remained friends through the thick and thin until his death in 2006. He was Uncle Lenny to my two girls, and I was godfather to his two boys.

Most of the men in my extended family were in the Navy during the second world war. My cousin, Ralph, who lived only two blocks from me, and who I idealized all my young life had been a ball turret gunner on a Grumman torpedo bomber, and fought in the battle of midway. He built model airplanes so I built model airplanes. My Mother always pushed me towards him, "be more like Ralph," she would say. I even took a picture of him to show and tell in second grade and told of his war adventures.

So the Navy was for me, and besides the Korean War was still going on and I already had my draft card. I thought the Navy would be safer. Little did I know of the dangers I would face.

I started out with many strikes against me. I was a left handed changed to be right handed with dyslexia which was unknown in the thirties.

My mother worked for the school district and I was suppose to start kindergarten at 6 years of age because of my birthday, but my mother pulled some strings and started me in kindergarten at age 4. With all these problems I had a terrible time in school and thought I was dumb.

With no possibility of going to college the only future ahead for me was working in the iron ore mines of northern Minnesota, joining the Navy was my answer. It was a few days before high school graduation, and I signed up as a airmen high school recruit. It sounded good but I found out later it meant nothing.

I graduated on Friday and had to be at the Minneapolis Post Office Monday morning June 9, 1952. I came back from celebrating graduation, and with a ticket in hand I walked by the hospital where my mother was in for a operation. In those days children under age were not allowed to visit people because of the polio epidemic. So the best I could do was to wave goodbye to her in a second story window and then caught the Greyhound bus.

The Greyhound Bus Company started in my home town, when the mining company moved the town five miles south so they could mine the ore that was under the original town site. There was North Hibbing, and South Hibbing, and the bus company was started to drive people back and forth. I have fond memories of old North Hibbing because my grandparents lived there and I would visit them in there big old house, and also I was born there in a small hospital, but of course none of the town exists any more. When I was about fourteen years old I had a paper route and one of my customers was a man we all called Bus Andy, because he started the famous company. Now there is a museum honoring him and the bus company in Hibbing.

In boot camp at Great Lakes, Illinois, we were given a multitude of tests, and all of a sudden I wasn't dumb anymore. I was offered to go to "Naval Cadet Air Training" this was the Navy school for pilots and I thought it would be great to learn to fly.

Great Lakes Naval Training Center is located on Lake Michigan about twelve miles south of the Wisconsin border. The train station separated the main side by the lake from the boot camp across the tracks. The first thing they did was give us about a ten second buzz cut. We then striped down and our clothes were sent back home, and a complete set of official clothing was litterally thrown at us as we walked by with our arms out stretched. We did a lot of marching mainly to different classes, we learned seaman ship, how to tie knots, and we had to be able to swim. We would jump in a pool take off our pants, tie knots in the legs and form a flotation device.

We were given old Springfield rifles. We had to use them in target practice, and take them apart and clean them. If you were caught calling your rifle a gun the Chief would stand you outside the barracks naked with a fart sack over you (mattress cover) holding a rifle and saying, "this is my rifle," then pointing down saying, "this is my gun, this is for fighting this is for fun".

This would go on for about three hours. Boot camp lasted twelve weeks, and after six weeks we were given a twelve hour liberty. A boot camp friend of mine, who lived in Chicago called has girlfriend, she brought a date for me and we wondered around the city sight seeing.

Chicago wasn't totally new to me. When I was one year old my parents took me to the 1934 Chicago World's Fair, and my mother told me that I saw John Dillinger. They had him laid out and a long line moved by to see the notorious bank robber. My mother told me she was shocked to see he had his toe nails painted.

Then twelve years later I returned by train to Chicago to stay for a couple of weeks with my aunt and cousins who had been visiting in northern Minnesota. We got to the train station downtown Chicago on the day the Second World War ended, it was quite the mess with celebrating everywhere, and we had a difficult time getting to their house. My cousin who was the same age as me and a bunch of his friends decided to go over to Wrigley Field "Cubs Park" to a baseball game. They had a way of sneaking in on the back side of the ticket booth. We would boost one another up to the roof on the booth, then over the wall and into the bleachers. I was first up and they caught us and down I came. We then proceeded to a different booth and tried again, because I was first up last time I was told I had to be last. Little did I know last didn't get into the game because there was nobody to boost you up. So I stood in the street hoping to pick up home run balls ,and of course none came.

The rest of time went by fast with my cousin playing stickball, a game called around the block, and trip to the Museum of Science and Industry where I still remember seeing a nine month display of babies in a bottle. Finally I was put on a train and my aunt asked a man to watch over me and back home I went.

Two weeks after my boot liberty in Chicago I received another liberty day for singing in the Blue Jacket Choir. This time I went alone to Milwaukee not knowing what to do, and finding out there really wasn't much for me to do being under age and only having a few hours to bum around downtown Milwaukee.

In Great Lakes we lived in our sea bags. This was a large round canvas bag that everything you owned could be packed in. All your clothes had to be rolled very tight and tied with a white cord. I doubt that sailors today know anything about this but in old movies a sailor could be seen with a seabag over his shoulder going aboard a ship.

In order to graduate from boot camp there was a sea bag inspection. All your clothes had to be rolled and tied one inch from each end with a white cord. So everyone re-rolled everything in their bag the night before the inspection. But lucky me I had to stand fire watch, (this is where you walk around for four hours while everyone is sleeping to protect agents possible fires), so I didn't get a chance to do my bag. After lights out I took my sea bag to the laundry room where I could turn on the lights not wake anyone up, and rolled my things. While busy rolling my stuff and not watching I kicked a stack of pails the top one tumbled and landed on my big toe. It hurt like hell, but I couldn't make a sound because the rest of my company was sleeping.

It swelled up by morning I was barely able to get my shoe on, but I past inspection and limped all the way home on boot leave.

I had to give the Navy a decision on going to "Nav Cad" when I got back. While at home I ran into a school friend who was also home on leave and had been in the Navy for a few years. He said "you don't want to be a pilot you will never get out of the service. If another war starts they will call you back in".

When I got back to boot camp I said "no" to Nav Cad, I'll do my four years get out and with the G.I. bill go to college.

Coming back from boot leave I took the train from Duluth, Minnesota, to Great Lakes, Illinois.

I was on the train with one other of my class mates who was from Northern Wisconsin. This was an evening train that would get us to the base in the early morning. I asked the conductor why it took twelve hours to go 400 miles? He told us this was a mail train and we stop at different hubs where the mail is loaded on to be brought to Chicago which is the main hub and that the passengers are just along for the ride. We were all alone sitting in the last car, while wondering through the train we noticed there were two good looking girls sitting in the car ahead of us. We said to them, " you should go and sit in the next car". They said "why," we told them because we are there. A little while later they came and joined us. They were secretaries from Chicago and a few years older then us in their early twenties.

The train stopped in a town where there was a night club just off the station platform with a band going strong. We asked the conductor how long we would be stopping," about 30 minutes," he said. We jumped off the train and went dancing when the whistle blew we headed back. The conductor said he has been doing this route for 30 years, and that was the first time it's ever happened. We got the girls phone numbers but I never called them back.

Because of my high scores on the tests I took in boot camp I was given a choice of schools. I picked electronic school, but first there was airman prep school in Norman, Oklahoma, for three months.

This was a school to cover all the different jobs the Navy had and also more tests. The higher the scores the better chance to get the school you wanted. Again the Navy lied to me I didn't have electronic school, but luckily my grades were good enough and I got to pick it anyway.

The school had just opened and there weren't even fences around the grounds. If you wanted to leave all you had to do was walk across the University of Oklahoma, which was right next door with just a golf course separating the prep school.

The school was so new that they didn't even have all the eating utensils in the chow hall so you did everything with a spoon.

We went on liberty in Oklahoma City which was only 17 miles away on the weekends. The Navy was new to the area and the girls really chased after us it was great. There was a large dance hall on the second floor of a building on Broadway and that became our hangout. I met a little red head from Seminole there and dated her most of the time I was there. We also hung out at the "Little White Cloud", it was a beer hall, hard liquor was illegal in Oklahoma but you could by a bottle from the hotel doorman. I saw the bottles they were selling it looked like they used old bottles over and over again I wasn't sure what was in them. We never bought any from the doorman.

One of my buddies came up to me on night borrowed twenty dollars and was going to hire a prostitute. Many hours later when he didn't show up we got worried, and went looking for him. We found the bellhop that had made the arrangements. "He is on the second floor raising hell, and the manager is calling the cops," we were told. When we got to the second floor here he is running down the hall in his shorts drunk and screaming at the top of his lungs, "I spent all your guy's money," when he saw us. We got him out of there quickly before the hotel manager called the cops.

We would rent a room at "Little Louie's Hotel" they didn't watch very carefully so the whole crew would sleep there. We would flip a coin for the bed, the couch, as well as for the pillows and blankets. It would be so crowded in the room we could hardly move. There was no way to get past all the bodies lying all over the place, let alone open the door and go down the hall to the toilet. So if we were desperate we used the window and the alley below. We were some of the first sailors in Oklahoma City, and it made this a great liberty town.

The only other time I have ever been to Oklahoma City was in 2002. My wife and I were driving to my high school reunion and we stopped there for the night. The next morning before going farther we drove down town to the Alfred P. Murrah National Memorial for the famous bombing. This was one of the most moving experiences of my life. We even dipped our hand in oil and left our hand print on a existing wall. Of all the memorials I have been to this was the best and the most moving and you couldn't walk away with a dry eye.

Throughout my service days my timing was great, the squadron went to was the first early warning squadrons based in Hawaii Barbers Point had just re-opened we were one of the first squadrons to be there. The base in Atsugi, Japan, had also not been used that long and we were one of the first squadrons there as well. A year after I left the squadron in, 1957 they moved VW-1 to Guam. The mission of the squadron had changed instead of a early warning assignment that became unpractical because of advancements in electronic surveillance. Now the squadron was called a weather reconnaissance squadron, and used for aerial hurricane surveillance. So I was almost the first and almost the last at both duty stations. The Navy said that Guam was more centrally located, and they could eliminate a detachment to Atsugi, and Barbers point. Also the Navy detachment in Okinawa had to open for our mission. It just seemed that a lot of places and things I did were the first or close to being the first ones, or the last or almost the last.

CHAPTER 2
ELECTRONIC SCHOOL

It was late November 1952 and I was on a train ride to Millington, Tennessee, to electronic school for twenty-six weeks.

Millington was about fifteen miles north of Memphis, the base about three miles east of the small town. It was winter and I thought it was cold in northern Minnesota, but with the dampness I never was as cold in my life as I was in Tennessee. It didn't matter how many layers of clothes you had on the cold would go right through. Back home the winters may be below zero, but they were so dry you couldn't even make snowballs.

I remember walking a post watch, this is where they would give you a belt with a night stick and a rifle and you would walk around a designated area for four hours to protect the area. The post watch I was assigned to was a 100 yard square area with one building in the center; it was the officers' club and they were having their Christmas party. There I was freezing for four hours supposedly protecting this building full of drunks. They would come out on the porch wave to me and laugh then go back in for some more fun.

In school we repaired radio and radar equipment back then there were no printed circuits no transmitters it was all wire and tubes in the radar hundreds of tubes. We would run the problem down to a specific area and start testing tubes because they were ninety percent of the problem. We built a radio, learned morse code, and flew radar training flights up and down the Mississippi in a two engine beachcraft.

On one of our radar training flights we were ready to take off when we were held up so a jet two seat training plane could take off. We heard a loud explosion and after a long wait we were given clearance to go. I saw a large burnt area out my window where the plane had just exploded. Another time the commander of the base was flying to get his flight time in. He was flying a Grumman Barracuda which was a over powered rotary engine plane with a short wing span and fast. There was just one problem, when the plane was at stalling speed it was dangerous because the large engine could cause the plane to flip over. Well on landing this happened he landed on the cockpit and was killed.

Memphis was a fun town, the southern bells just loved the Navy and dates were easy to get. I started to date a student nurse. Then there was a secretary that I met at the USO dance and went with her most of the time I was there. The drinking age was 18 and I think I tried every kind of drink there was, this was something new to a young guy from Minnesota. Often this lead to dangerous results and the USO furnished bunks for fifty cents a night, so it was easy to head for a bunk when things got fuzzy. It was a great place to be stationed.

I met a student nurse at the USO dance. We dated for a while but that didn't last because they had to be in the dorm by 9 pm.

This wasn't my only encounter with student nurses. Years later while attending Junior collage on the GI Bill back home Lenny, I, and five of our friends would date the students that came up to Hibbing for special training. They stayed at the YWCA and did not have many restrictions. So it was party time, and when they would head back to school they would leave notes to the incoming class with our group's phone number.

I don't know what they said but the new group would always contact us. We would pick up the new group and all of us would go dancing at the bar thirteen and everyone would pare up. Dale's parents would not use their lake cabin in the winter so we would go there for parties. One time there was a party of about 30 people when all of a sudden lights appeared in the night sky. Everyone ran through the woods to where the lights came from. There we found a car turned upside down in the deep snow still running, with the wheels still turning, and one of our buddies still in the drivers seat. We pulled him out, he was okay but drunk. He had gone down to a bar a mile down the road he missed a curve on his way back, flipped over, and slid in the snow. The next day we all went over and tipped the car back up. He washed it off it was in perfect condition and he drove it home. It was one of those cars from the fifties a Nash torpedo back with unit body construction, they made cars a lot stronger in those days.

At Christmas time we were given two weeks leave to go home. I caught a ride from one of the guys and he dropped me off at the train station downtown Chicago. There were no trains going north until the next day so I decided to try the bus. I walked out of the station and asked a cabby where the Greyhound station was he said, "I will take you there but I won't tell you". I gave him a few dollars and jumped in where he drove me around the corner and there was the bus station, I got taken.

In the station I ran into a table full of my high school classmates all heading to Hibbing for Christmas. One was even a future sister-in-law, but of course didn't know that at the time. After about an hour of good conversation the bus came and home we all went.

When I got home I found out that Lenny was home on leave at the same time, so I had someone to chum around with.

He was serving on the battleship Missouri, and was just back from the Mediterranean. It was great visiting with his folks. His dad was like a second father to me, and always took us hunting and fishing. I never shot anything hunting, and I was the worlds worst fisherman.

After Christmas I headed by bus back to Memphis. I was surprised when the bus stopped on the Kentucky border and the bus driver stated all blacks to the back of the bus, this was one of the first times I came across racism.

When I got back a friend/classmate bought an old Chevy for two hundred dollars, the dealer gave my buddy and I each a calendar with Marilyn Monroe laying on red velvet, this was on the inside of my locker for the year.

My buddy was from Belleville, Illinois, and wanted to head home to show off his new car. So four of us sold blood to get money and took off on a vampire liberty for the weekend. There is one incident that reminds me of our trip. We were at a restaurant sitting in a window seat, I had a mixed drink I brought into the restaurant, when the waitress came up to me and told me no liquor is allowed. I went outside to throw it away, when I noticed a car outside our window. I put my drink on the hood of the car and went back into the restaurant. The next thing I knew one of the guys said "there goes your drink." The car pulled out with my drink still on the hood and was driving down the street. I took off running down the street when the car stopped at a red light. I ran up to the car, my drink was still on the hood, I grabbed my drink you never have seen such a startled person.

I bought an old 1940 Cadillac coupe as my love machine. It had Arkansas plates the dealer had put on the car and there was no title. It couldn't be registered so I got it for fifty bucks, I had a car for as long as I was stationed there, but it was illegal. I always thought I could get a clear title but that never happened. We met most of our dates at the USO in downtown Memphis, one of our places we liked to go on weekends was a man made lake with a sandy beach where we could lay around and get a tan. One time we went to Blue Lake it was across the bridge in Arkansas it was a back wash for the Mississippi River. When we got there we noticed a life guard seating in town with a rifle, I asked him what was he doing with a rifle. He told me he was watching for water moccasin snakes. It wasn't that great of a place with muddy water, we never went back.

One time after a date it was about two o'clock in the morning and I was headed back to the base. We always took the back roads because it was a lot shorter. It was an old two lane road that ran through a swampy area on both sides of the road. I was driving and I could see the traffic signal at the intersection in Millington, and at the light is where you would take a right to head down to the base. The light was red and I stopped. The next thing I knew I woke up with the car running and sitting in the middle of the road miles from Millington with the dark murky water on both sides. How long I was sitting there? I have no idea, but It was a good thing the light was red in my dream or I would have driven right into the swamp. I had a guardian angel that night.

My year was now up and my next assignment was North Island Naval Air Station, San Diego. I would be there for one year and then I would have to go to a squadron to serve my sea duty. So after a thirty day leave it would be off to California.

I drove home with my old caddie letting my dad try to use it for a trade in on a new car, but with no clear title the only thing we got for it was junk. When I was in boot camp I got a name of a gal in Wisconsin from my friend we became pen pals. So while I was home I borrowed my dad's car for a few days and drove over to meet with Donna. We got along great and our meeting solidified a relationship. She was a secretary and had graduated the same year I did; we went dancing and went to the movie Brigadoon, which remains one of my favorite movie to this day, because later I was on the set where it was made ,and walked among the heather when I took a USO tour of the studio.

I headed back home from Wisconsin thinking I was in love. The song Donna was playing on the radio and I hummed the tune thinking of our few days together. The rest of my time home flew by and it was time to head back because I was being transferred. The Navy supplied me with a train ticket to Los Angles, and then a bus ticket to San Diego..

CHAPTER 3
SAN DIEGO
FOR A YEAR

North Island Naval Air Station is located across the bay from San Diego on a peninsula that at one time probably was an island. When I was there in 1953 we had no bridge to get us over there you had to take a ferry to get to the town of Coronado and then the base. The other way to get there was by a boat called the Nickel Snatcher. I use to joke that it was the only boat I was on in four years in the Navy. Some times the ride across the bay became an experience. One time a drunken sailor walked off the wrong side of the boat. After pulling himself out of the water he started to strip and ring out his clothes, and all the waves aboard the boat stood around to watch the show.

I was stationed at base radio. We were in a concrete bunker in the center of the base, where all the transmitters were located. We had to keep them under repair and one of us had to be there around the clock. The entire radio building was located across the air strip next to the ocean. We would serve duty alternating between the two sites. We would find illegals who came across the border by our radio shack, and they were stuck there because North Island was a peninsula, and they could go no farther north. We worked eight hours on and eight hours off for two days and then had three days off. Because of our strange work times we were in an odd hour dorm right above the chow hall. We even had a special staircase and were able to go to the head of the chow line.

There was no wake up time the dorm was always dark because some men were always sleeping at all odd times. Along with the base radio men there firemen, the shore patrol, and the entertainers that all stayed in the dorm. The guy who slept above me was a base player who played with a group that was featured on the all service Ed Sullivan Show. It seemed that all the musicians know each other and he introduced me to Stan Kenton one time when we went to see him perform.

One of the guys a few bunks over named Dean Jones was a fireman, and he was asked to escort Miss San Diego around the base. He ended up marrying her, they went to Hollywood her career didn't take off, but he became a star in all the Disney "Herbie the Love Bug" movies. Another guy in the dorm was the chubby friend of the Nelson's in "Ozzie and Harriet."

San Diego was not a great liberty town if you were under twenty one, because you couldn't get into the night spots to dance and meet the girls. So on the three days off it was time to hitchhike up to Hollywood to the U.S.O.

Hitchhiking to L.A. was an experience all its own. There was only two freeways, the Santa Ana, and the Hollywood. Because it was almost impossible to hitch a ride on the freeway we would take highway number One up the coast to Long Beach and then western avenue up to Hollywood. I don't think traveling these streets with your thumb would be very safe now days.

The U.S.O. was located one block east of Hollywood and Vine. The U.S.O. would have tickets to radio and television shows one day Doug and I went on Truth and Consequences he made fifty bucks. He was from Michigan, and when the announcer had the Michigan State team that was there for the Rose Bowl game stand up he let out a yell. Art Linkletter said young man come on down. The next day we were in the U.S.O. watching the Rose Bowl game on T V when someone said they had two tickets to the Rose Bowl game. We grabbed the tickets and got on the next bus and we were on our way. We got to the Rose Bowl game but never made it to our seats, we watched the last two minutes of the game at least I can say I was at a Rose Bowl game.

Many stars would come to the U.S.O. on Sunday night to dance with the service men and to serve us food. I danced with a young Rita Moreno her strap on her dress kept falling off her shoulders so she tore it off through it on the dance floor, and we continued to dance. One Saturday they would have movie studio tours I was able to watch many movies in the making like; *Rear Window, A Star is Born,* and *The Seven Little Foys.* On one of the movie studio tours I met Doris Day and Jerry Lewis. When I need to get some sleep the Y.M.C.A. had mattresses on the gym floor for fifty cents a night for service men.

One night a shipmate and I were able, for the one and only time, get into a night club in San Diego. The crowd was pushing at the entrance, and we got shoved past the bouncer. We met two girls much older then us went to one of their houses and spent part of the night. I stopped over the next day and visited ,Ginger, the gal I had been with, but that was as far as that relationship went. She was in the middle of a divorce, and had a young child, and at 19 years of age I didn't want to get mixed up in that mess.

One Sunday Garry and I decided to go to Catalina Island. So we boarded a launch and sailed of to the island. When we got there the place was wall to wall people, and parties going on all over the place. Because of our crazy work schedule we didn't pay much attention to the calendar. Here it was Memorial Day weekend the first big holiday of the season. There were no places to rent the island was full up. So we rolled up in newspapers and slept on the beach along with many other poor souls. The next day people started to leave heading home for work, and we found a room for the night.

We met two very pretty girls, and enjoyed their company for the rest of the time we were there. The girl I was with said that she really wanted to see the movie *Rebel Without a Cause*. I knew it was playing at the Paramount up in Hollywood, and offered to take her to the show the next weekend.

I hitchhiked up to L.A. gave a taxi driver her address and I was on my way. When the taxi pulled up to the address I gave him I thought this must be a mistake, here was this humongous old mansion. When I got out I felt like getting back in the cab and leave as I was confronted by a pair of extremely large oak doors. I pulled a large wooden handle attached to rope and a large gong nearly knocked me out of my shoes.

I could tell that the family was not glad to see there daughter dating a sailor, and threw dozens of questions at me. They gave strict orders for her to be back right after the movie. What kind of date is this going to be I thought, I'm just a way for her to get out to see a movie.

She paid the taxi, and we jumped in her bright red chevy convertible and off to the movies we went. After the movie she left me on Hollywood boulevard and drove home. I was just a convenience for the night, a way for her to get out of the house to see the movie.

I hung around with a bunch of shipmates from New York. It was the time of DA haircuts, pet pants, and dancing the bop. We would go to Tijuana Mexico to dance with the stripers, they were the best dancers. They would sometimes bring back marijuana. I tried it once, but I had a terrible coughing spell and found out that the weed was not for me.

One time in Tijuana while waiting for a friend to come out of a bar I put my foot on a bumper of a taxi cab. All of a sudden the taxi cab driver came running and screaming that I was damaging his car, and pointed to a old dent in his bumper. By this time my friend had returned and the taxi cab driver was calling the police. We jumped into another taxi and headed for the border. A police car started to chase us we reached the US side just in the knick of time, sliding sideways across the border.

One of the guys I was stationed with had met the Moray Dancers who were entertaining with Bob Hope and the San Diego Fair.

One of our groups had rented a beach house because he was planning on getting married so we had a house warming party. We invited the Moray Dancers and it was a great party with nude midnight swimming. Because of all the noise we made the next day he lost his lease. We stopped over the next afternoon to visit some of the dancers at there motel. They said "last night was fun but we all have lives up in Hollywood, and don't need any more complications.

Well my time was up at North Island and it was time for sea duty. Lucky the Korean War had just ended so my sea duty would not be so dangerous at least that's what I thought.

I was going home on leave and thought about seeing my pen pal from Wisconsin when I got my one and only "Dear John" letter, so no more trips to Wisconsin. The old saying is true, "Distance makes the heart grow fonder for someone else".

Chapter 4
Going To Hawaii

My assignment for sea duty was VW-1 I in Barbers Point Hawaii. All I knew about the squadron was that it was new and was just formed a few years ago. First I had to use up some of my leave so I caught a hop from a Navy plane going to the Midwest. There was a good looking wave aboard and she was flirting with the pilots. We were a few hours out when the word was passed back saying that we were going to land in Albuquerque for the night. The next morning there was no pilots and no wave so I and a fellow passenger going to Wisconsin saw a plane ready to take off. Where are you going we asked? "Milwaukee," was the answer, so we hopped aboard and got closer to home. This was an Admiral's private plane, and very plush inside, so we traveled in the lap of luxury. From Milwaukee I used my thumb to get to northern Minnesota. It wasn't easy getting home it was winter, and I was hitch hiking from a small town in the middle of Wisconsin. I went in a gas station to get warm. There was a guy there getting some work done on his car he said, "I don't give rides to hitchhikers, but I will make an exception for you," so when the car was finish off we went to Minneapolis. It was to cold to hitchhike any further so I took a bus to Duluth, but first I calling my parents to pick me up.

"Wake up," my dad said, here I was asleep in the back of the bus. The bus had stopped in Duluth and all the passengers had gotten off. The bus was going to return to the garage when my dad said, "my son should be on that bus let me look," and he found me.

After two weeks at home my parents brought me to Minneapolis Navy facility, and there was a hop going to Ogden, Utah. I grabbed it atleast it would get me half way to San Francisco. We landed in Ogden and as we were taxing in another plane was preparing to take off. My pilot shouted out the window to the other pilot, "Where are you going?" the answer back was" San Francisco." "I have a passenger for you," my pilot told him. The pilot from the other plane said "no way," but as my pilot pointed to his captain bars on his shoulder he told him yes he would. So I switched planes on the runway and I thought to myself San Francisco here I come. This was a pretty good day of traveling especially in the fifties. I had left home in northern Minnesota in the morning, and here I was checking into Treasure Island Naval Station that evening.

Treasure Island was half way from San Fran to Oakland on the Bay Bridge. This was a Navy transfer station where they would process your papers, and arrange transportation. Treasure Island is a mostly manmade Island that was used for the World's Fair. After that it became the home base for the China Clipper [the large flying boat] then left idle until the Navy took it over. While you were there waiting to be shipped out shit details were the job of the day. I was assigned to the butcher shop. We were given a large side of beef and with a sharp knife told to cut out anything red and throw it into a large bucket about three feet across. Then we were to cube up the fat and throw this in a different bucket. The butcher in charge would take a shovel and mixed red and white together. We protested about how terrible that was to do, his reply was "this was the best hamburger you can get, and it was getting made for the officers mess hall."

On my time off I first took liberty in San Francisco. I wondered around downtown, and then rode the cable car to Fisherman's Warf, and then headed back to the base on the A train.

The next time I had liberty I decided to go to Oakland. I liked it much better, it was a smaller place, and all the bars were located in one area. I went bar hopping, but being alone it wasn't much fun, so I was ready to head back to the base, when this not so very good looking woman came over and became very friendly. I wasn't interested in her and said "I have to get back to the base," I lied and said "I have the duty." She said that they, and pointed to a well dressed man standing near by, would give me a ride to the base. The man came over and handed me a limp hand to shake. I didn't feel right about the situation and begged off, but they insisted so reluctantly I went along, saying because I had the duty and had to get back in a hurry. I got in a big new Lincoln, and off we went. They mentioned a party the next night. I lied, and told them that I would bring all of my buddies to the party. That seemed to ease the situation, what they didn't know being in transit I didn't know anyone. When I was safely back inside the base I thought, "What a scary situation," but my lie saved the day. I think the man could have been a woman, and the woman could have been a man, I hope they don't get to disappointed when know one shows up for their orgy.

A few days later a bus took me to Travis Air Force Base where I got on a plane headed to Hawaii. We were a few miles off the coast when an engine caught on fire and we had to return back. Was this an omen of things to come I wondered?

The next day we took off again, and about a few hundred miles from Hawaii a steward came up to me. He was very worried and told me that the plane had no brakes, and they weren't sure if the wheels would come down either. I asked "why are you telling me this," his reply was because I had airman wings on my sleeve. I said, "Thanks, now I will have to worry all the way to Hawaii." He said that he would let me know if things improve. As we approached Hawaii I heard the wheels come down and felt relieved.

We landed at Hickam Field, but because we had no brakes we coasted to the far side of the Honolulu International Airport, the runways were connected, another omen maybe. We were miles from the base and we were towed back at 5 miles an hour. It was hot about 90 degrees and with high humidity. I don't remember a worse couple of hours sitting in the sweltering plane, but at least I am here and ready to meet my squadron.

CHAPTER 5
MY SQUADRON

IT Was August, 1954 a bus took me to Barbers Point Naval Air Station. It is located as far west from Honolulu as you can get by the town of Ewa Beach, and during the Second World War was called Ewa Field. The Navy had recently taken it over and when I got there they were still building barracks. We were housed in temporary barracks it was a long two story quonset with all the enlisted men on the base housed there while ours were being renovated after sitting empty for a long time.

When I arrived there were only two squadrons a P2V group and ours. Every thing was spread out and it was a long walk to get anywhere. This was to protect everything from potential Japanese bombs because the base had been attacked with Pearl Harbor. Because of the distances, the first thing to do was buy a car. I went in halves on a 1938 Buick for $150 it was rusty black, and looked like a gangster's car. Everyone was driving old rusty cars because the Navy would only ship newer cars when you got transferred so the old rusty hulks were left, and getting rustier by the day with the high humidity. I remember in one friend's car the floor was rusted out and you could see the road go by between your feet.

VW-1 was an early warning squadron its insignia was Paul Revere riding with a lantern. "One if by land and two if by sea." This was the historic signal for alert in the revolutionary war years of 1776. This was sufficient then, but in the twentieth century it has become necessary to find an invader and give the alert as soon as possible.

With atomic laden aircraft flying faster then the speed of sound, an entirely new concept of preliminary warning of impending attack has come into existence, making Paul Revere's lantern obsolete.

The squadron was started to prevent another sneak attack like Pearl Harbor. The idea was that these would be flying radar stations scanning the sky to give this early warning. We were the first and because of that no one really knew what were supposed to do, we were the miss fits that no one really wanted. So the squadron would make up jobs to keep the planes flying in the two years I was in VW-1 we never did the job that was the assignment. That was to fly a post back and forth looking for the enemy.

The Squadron

When I first arrived at the squadron they had some old B-17 Second World War bombers, a few Super Connie, and a baby connie which was a shorter version of the Super Constellation. These were fixed out like radar planes with a large radar dome on the top and bottom. I only had one flight in the B-17 and I remember it was cold and the skin of the plane was thin. I wondered how the crew survive on bombing runs during the second world war, bullets would just go through like paper, the only protection I could see was the pilot had a hunk of metal under his seat.

I was an airman third class and because I was not a petty officer I was required to do three months of shit duty a year usually compartment cleaning, mess hall, and this time I was sent to base radio, so I officially did not become a member of the squadron till November 14,1954.

Our duties were to keep contacts with all the planes flying out of Barbers Point for local flights we used Morris code, and for flights to other areas (called Transpacking) voice was used, this was great for me it me to improve my code. You had to get so it was sent counting dots and dashes but putting them together to form words, and if you weren't fast enough you could not become part of a flight crew. That was the main objective for all new members of the squadron, because if you fly you get flight skins that is an extra $100 a month. That doesn't sound like much these days but 50 years ago it was a different story.

While I was at base radio the squadron started to send B-17's back to Burbank, California, and after a few weeks returning with a brand new Super Constellation radar domes on top and bottom.

Executives from Lockheed and Trans World Airlines met in 1939 to design a 50 passenger aircraft with a maximum cruising speed of 300 miles per hour. In a attempt to attain maximum aerodynamic efficiency, the Constellation was designed with the three vertical tails, one of the distinctive trademarks in aviation. No commercial production of the Connie was built prior to Pearl Harbor, but after that fifteen were constructed for the Air Force, and called the C-69. After the Second World War a total of 50 were manufactured in a span of 15 years up to 1957, divided equally between the military, and the commercial airlines. When I was in VW-1 we had Connie's numbers one through seven.

The crew would come back with all the tales of liberty in Hollywood and everyone listened to every word hoping they would be the next crew to go. This wasn't such a big deal for me I had spent a year in San Diego and hitchhiked up to Hollywood almost every weekend. I met a lot of girls at the U.S.O. I dated a model for a while, Jonie modeled clothing at a large department store on Hollywood Boulevard.   She lived just a few blocks up the street from the USO, and I spent Christmas with her and her family.   One day I ran into her father on the street we had a long talk about his daughter, and he made me promised that I would not take advantage of her.   Later on we broke up when she took off with one of my friends, and later I heard that he got her pregnant.   I guess he didn't make the same promise.   Then there was a starlet, she was under contract with a studio but she hadn't worked in a picture yet.   I don't think she ever did work in a picture.

There was a bar at the corner of Hollywood and Vine it was famous because all the caricature drawings framed on the wall.   I was able to get in the bar because I typed a zero and placed it over the three on my ID card with spit.   It made me three years older, and if they asked to see the card out of my wallet I would just rub off the zero as I pulled it out.   It worked perfect in fact on Catalina Island a bartender said it was such a good job that he served me anyway.

Well at the bar I met a tall beautiful redhead she said her name was Roma she was Italian from northern Italy.   She was in the movie business and invited me and my friend Larry to a party the next night. Well Larry and I hailed a cab gave the address and to the party we went. It was a house in the Hollywood hills. Roma vouched for us and we were in. There must have been more that a hundred people there and the house was the most unusual I had ever seen. There were numerous floors with just a few rooms on each with an enormous large main room on the first floor. I am not sure if I met any important people that night but it was a great party.

So going back to Burbank to get a plane was not that big of a deal for me, but I still wouldn't have minded going back for a visit. My main objective for now was getting out of base radio and being assigned to a plane crew.

By this time I was a petty officer third class that is an eagle with one red stripe below before this I had three green stripes. These ranks were not just given to you, you had to earn them first you had to have time in rank then get an appointment from the commanding officer. All this so you could just take the test. So you can say the rank was not just given to you.

Chapter 6
The Plane

When I left base radio and reported back to the squadron I was assigned to number 4 as a second radio operator and first ECM operator (Electronic Counter Measures). Plane #4 was unique it was the only gray super Connie. All the rest were silver we called it the grey ghost. The Super Connie was the most beautiful plane made in its day it consisted of four Prat in Whitney Motors and it had three tails with a large radar dome on top and a big round one on its belly it flew at 300 miles per hour. It carried a large amount of fuel in the wings and in two wing tanks. We could stay up for a long time and fly all the way to Hawaii from Japan.

My Plane

The giant plane could perform many duties, such as search and rescue missions, reconnaissance, weather observation, and submarine detection. When necessary cameras recorded any pictures on the radarscope for future reference.

One of my best friends in VW-1 was a radar operator on our plane. He came into the squadron the same day I did and got discharged at the same time. We became fast friends and bummed around everywhere together. In later years our families got together many times, but sadly Sunding died in 1995.

In the Navy the plane and crew stay together this is your crew this is your plane you cleaned it you repaired it you kept it flying. The only problem with this comradery is that you get to know your crew like a family, and of course there was typical family disputes but like a family everyone stuck together. You didn't get to know the other crews that well because planes were always going to different places all the time, like ships passing in the dark. Once every six months the crew would get together and gunk the plane, which is to brush on a thick solution called gunk and then hose it off it would take all day to finish. Now the plane was nice and clean and it was said it would fly faster. Of course the officers did not get the opportunity to have all this fun.

The plane consisted of 14 crew members two mechanics, one was the crew chef, two electricians, four radio men, two pilots, two co-pilots, and two navigators. We also had six radar operators who were our passengers and not part of the crew. We also had five ground crew who were assigned to our plane but they didn't fly. Because of the long flight hours and range, the plane was maintained by a crew of well trained technicians. All officers must be graduates of the combat information center school in Glenview, Illinois. The pilots are all veteran air transport pilots with thousands of hours at the controls of multi-engine aircraft. The flight engineers are trained for emergencies, and around them revolves the entire safety of the aircraft.

On the plane first came the cockpit including the pilots, and flight engineer who sat at the large board showing how the engines are running, then came the galley where the food was cooked. All the food was brought on uncooked we would eat steak with all the trimmings and a lot of other items including chicken. On the day they would have chicken I would beg not to have chicken, and they would make a hamburger for me. When I was four years of age I was on a farm and they were going to have chicken. They cut its head off and the headless chicken chased me all around the farm yard. I haven't been able to eat any chicken since the traumatizing event. Our electrical engineer did all the cooking and he was a great chef. There were two booths for eating playing cards and drinking coffee.

Next on the plane came the navigators on one side of the isle, and the radio station on the other side, right behind the radio desk were some large ducts that high frequency radar signals traveled through. It was thought that all the high frequency running right behind our backs would make us sterile but I had no problems in my 50 years since. Then came all the radar stations and across the row were the sleeping bunks just like a train, upper and lowers. The toilets were next they consisted of a large metal box with a seat on top, to empty it we lowered it through a hatch onto the bottom of the plane, then when we could we would carry the metal boxes to a toilet to dump. Needless to say it was a very stinky job. On remote landing stripes we would just fertilize the ground next to the runway. Also on the back wall there was a urinal that emptied into space. Many a time I peed on Waikiki beach, but it evaporated before it reached the ground, but it was fun saying I peed on Waikiki. Nobody was fond of us anyway, the signs would say dogs and sailors keep off the grass. So with that feeling toward servicemen to look for a date we would check out the tourists.

CHAPTER 7
HAWAII

You have to realize this was 50 years ago I am sure things have changed by now. A local girl would not be caught with a service man. That was a total no! In fact they would probably be disowned. One has to realize that a young man of 19 was more interested in the girl situation on Hawaii then the beautiful scenery.

I went to a dance for service men there were 400 men and 25 hostesses. You were tagging a guy to break into dance and there were four guys at the same time tagging each other to break in for a dance. It was a joke to say the least. We did meet some tourists and dated them while they were visiting. I told one gal that the enlisted men's symbol "E" on my car window stood for ensign which is an officer rank instead of an enlisted man.

Of course it wasn't the same Hawaii, there were only two hotels on Waikiki, the Royal Hawaiian and the Moana with it's banyan tree in the court yard. On Saturday afternoon on a low balcony in the court yard a radio show Hawaii Calls would be broadcasted to the United States.

There wasn't a lot of tourists it was mainly a service man town at that time. But about the time in 1956 when I left to come back to the big island (which is what we called the U. S. mainland) more hotels were starting to be built and the tourist trade was starting to pick up.

The battleship Arizona had only a small section above the water and the flag was raised every day from that section. If you didn't know it was there when you drove by on the highway you would miss it and it's importance to the bombing of Pearl Harbor. Now there is the beautiful Arizona Monument with boats to take the tourists to it and I have seen it both ways.

We would drive around the island but you can only do that so many times. We would go to Waimea Falls to get there was tough there were no roads you had to walk along a path by the river. I have a picture I took of one of my crew mates jumping off the falls feet first in his shorts. Of course this may not sound like a big thing, but there were many crosses painted on rocks honoring people who had died diving off the falls, of course they went head first. Now days it is Waimea Falls State Park and they have diving expeditions off the falls, but all the dangerous obstacles have been removed. We spent a lot of time swimming, skin diving, and saving money to spend in Japan.

Another hobby a group of us had was joining a photography club on the base. The guy in charge had been a professional photographer in Hollywood; and we would go on photo excursions around the island. This was great because Hawaii is loaded with photo opportunities.

One time he talked a Wave into posing for us. Sad to say she was not nude. He showed us all the tricks of model photo shooting and how to get the great shot. He would use clothes pins on the back of her skimpy clothing to make it tighter and more sexy.

You have to realize that this was 50 years ago. I have been back to Hawaii many times since then and was even married over there, I have a warm spot in my heart for the Islands now, but that was then.

CHAPTER 8
OUR MISSION

We were the first early warning squadron and because of that no one knew what to do with us. In the future there was a plan to have these planes flying a surveillance route around the United States to prevent another sneak attack like Pearl Harbor.

Remember flying years ago radar did not have a great range, there were no missiles, and there were no satellites in outer space to watch for us. We were the best idea at the time to keep our country safe from an enemy attack. However the Korean War was over so who was our enemy now? In the Pacific it was probably China.

So what was VW-1 to do? We flew around so everyone would get their flight time in, this was ten hours to get what we called flight skin. I don't know what the officers got for their flight hours, but the crew got $100 a month. I banked all my skin money and had a few thousand dollars when I got discharged and bought a car.

We did familiarize ourselves with the plane and its limitations, we checked the radio frequencies around the pacific, and we did fly rescue missions looking for down pilots. We never found one it was almost impossible to spot a life raft in the choppy ocean. Every white cap in the ocean water looked like a raft.

Once we flew to Midway Island for a few days. Why? They never told us. Midway Island actually was two islands one a barren rock the other housed the naval air station. I felt sorry for the sailors that were stationed at Midway. If they were lucky they would get a few weeks in Hawaii a year. The Navy had some lousy duty stations this was bad but not the worst there was always Kwajalein Island that everyone considered the pits at least on Midway there were the gooney birds to torment. The Gooney bird was actually a Black-footed Albatross, also known as Laysan Albatross, they were one of the greatest flying birds, but on land one of the clumsiest you would ever find, and that's how it got its name.

They were all over the islands by the thousands, and Midway was a bird sanctuary so you couldn't kill them. The guys stationed there would take a light bulb and swap it for an egg. Then when the bird sat on the bulb they would turn it on and watch the fire works when the bird burned its bottom.

Another trick they showed us was at the end of the runway all the birds would line up and take off one at a time, they would run and flap their gigantic wings until they were air born. When the birds were about six feet off the ground the guys would tip one wing with his hand. The bird would fall and roll head over heals down the runway then they would pick themselves up and go get in the back of the line and start all over again. We were glad to leave Midway never to return.

Now days Midway Island and it's adjoining coral reefs are part of the largest protected marine area in the world, and people are only allowed in to clean up the area. The Navy had used the Island for a base for decades, but left in 1996. In the future the Island will become a tourist destination, but only for less-disruptive activities such as swimming and snorkeling.

Another mission we went on was to fly up to the Aleutian Islands to check radio frequency in the winter. Because of the time of the year we were issued poopsie suits these were rubber suits now like the ones surfers wear. We were to wear them under our clothes and you can guess why they were called poopsie suits. The suit was given just in case we crashed into the freezing cold water without the suit you only had minutes to live. With the suit you had about fifteen minutes. Big deal I thought it is better to go quick instead of thinking about it for fifteen minutes. With all the flying we did by the time I got discharged I had over 2000 hours of flight time way more then I needed for my flight pay.

CHAPTER 9
OUR JAPANESE
DITACHMENT

By the time I joined the squadron from base radio detachment able was formed, and one crew was already making the arrangements.

Our main base was Barbers Point Hawaii now we had detachment able in Japan, and also we were given a section of the air force base Naha Okinawa for detachment baker.

The plan now was to send three planes to Japan for three months at a time and they would also be using Naha. So our rotation was three months Japan, six months Hawaii, back and forth with one plane rotating out each month. The saying was save your money in Hawaii and spend it in Japan.

Atsugi was the base in Japan it was the air strip MacArthur landed at when the war ended. It also was the Kamikaze Base where they trained and took off for there last flight. Kamikaze or "Divine Wind" pilots were named after a legendary typhoon that foiled the Mongol Emperor Kublai Kahn's invasion of Japan in 1281. There were a estimated 4000 pilots at two training bases of which over 95% died in the war. Wheels were rigged to fall off the planes on takeoff, there was no turning back. Diaries show that rather then stoic warriors many of them were tortured souls flying to there death.

When the war ended the pilots who hadn't killed themselves were scared to leave the base they were disowned by their families they were suppose to die for the Empire so they stayed on base. When the Navy took Atsugi over, they were still there, so the Navy hired them to work on the base. They were the mess cooks, compartment cleaners, and did all the odd jobs around. They felt unworthy and disgraced, we use to tell them aren't you lucky we came along and saved your life. All the buildings were left over from there time there was even a Shinto Shrine on the base for there use.

Astugi Main Gate

Atsugi was not to far from Mount Fuji this is the Japanese sacred mountain. You could look up across the air field and there it was in all its snow caped beauty. It was a wonderful site to see every morning. The base was located about twenty miles from Yokohama which was our closest large city and where we went to shop. Tokyo was about thirty-five miles away, and everything in Japan was real close, trains were fast and always on time so it didn't take long to get to anywhere. The base was large with a golf course running around the outside. Across the runways was a marine detachment they were next to the town of Atsugi. On our side was a small town just outside the main gate called Sagami-Otsuka, it was built as a party town for the kamikaze pilots where they could have their last fling before they took their last flight. There were 61 bars in Sagami-Otsuka and a train station. Across the track from the main town was the bar Fuji this was a large building with a second floor this was built for the high ranking Japanese Officers. Calling them bars was not a true description they were a place where you could eat, drink, or spend the night. They were not very large usually a Mama-san would be in charge with three girls working for her it was like a small home away from home.

When our first plane returned from Japan we were all eager to hear about their adventure it sounded extremely exciting and we all looked over the pictures they brought back which made everyone more excited to go.

One of the things brought back from Japan were 10 yen coins. I discovered they were the same size as a quarter. I tried one in the juke box on the base, but It fell straight through it was to light. So I spit on the coin and tried it again, this time it worked music started playing. The word got around and soon everyone was spitting on the 10 yen coins and bringing them back by the pocket full. Needless to say the owner of the coin machines on base could not make any money at 3 ½ cent for a quarter so he took all the coin machines off the base.

When I got discharged and was traveling through Reno I tried some 10 yen coins in a one armed slot machine they worked but of course I didn't win anything.

It was two more months before it was my turn turn to go to Japan. We packed up and took off with excitement. We landed in Guam and gassed up and continued on our way Atsugi – here we come.

CHAPTER 10
MY FIRST TRIP
TO JAPAN

When I arrived at Atsugi they were still setting up the base. The Japanese workman were building a docking facility for us. It was made out of heavy bamboo and all tied together with rope. I was very impressed on the quality of the work and how steady it was it enabled the mechanics and electricians to reach all parts of the plane wings and engines for repairs. Most of the time we tube tested first and most of the problems were solved, there were no transistors or printed circuit boards in those days.

In 1945 in the early days of the occupation of Japan it was a common thing for service men to give candy to the kids, now ten years later those eight year olds are now eighteen and beautiful Japanese women with a kind spot in their heart for American service men. It was love at first sight for both the guys and the Josans (this was a name we called the girls along with a more personal name of Babysan). Who is a Babysan or a JoSan? let me give you a brief description of this phenomenon that only happened for maybe ten years, form the time of the Korean War or say from 1948 to 1958. Before this the Japanese were still reeling from the end of the war, the JoSans were young children who got a favorable opinion of the kind US service men, and after about 1960 the country became very sophisticated. Young women were now going to college and entering into the work force. Service men who were there in those days know exactly what I am talking about it was a moment in time that happened once and will never happen again.

The world of Babysan, came with the occupation of Japan a carefree charming girl she never forgot the kindness of the G.I. and she would make the stay in Japan a pleasant one. In appearance she seemed tiny but not a fragile doll, her face is oval her cheekbones high her nose is pug with her mouth pouting and hair dark and long. Compared to the American girls she is short and trim and with a heart as big as the great outdoors, she is both sensitive and practical and your wish is her command if reasonable. She has tried very hard to become westernized more American like in her makeup and dress. Sometimes she over does this a little in her giving to please the service man.

In her adopted manners and new way of life have given her a touch of individuality she is not the vision we were led to expect there are no kimonos not the famous Geisha girl from the movie *Sayonara* this type of women are still around and I would see them on trains and in the street but there not really seen chained to a sailor.

Few girls in the world are cleaner and neater always adding little touches to make her well groomed. She prefers to be different every time you see her she can do more with less and still look beautiful.

JoSan is smart and cleaver she has brains and uses them it is hard to outwit them. They may not have organized schooling but they are wise to the ways of the world and quick to pick things up even thou she will be careful to not appear too brilliant to make a boy friend fall in controls but she will get her way with out you knowing it.

So this is a brief description of Babysan you can see why the service men were so enamored with these fascinating young women.

Sagami

Josan

Chesico

The Shinto Shrine

Eleanor Roosevelt dropped by Japan after the war and was appalled at all the service men fraternizing with the girls. She got the commanding officer of the pacific to order the main gate of all bases in Japan will be closed from midnight to seven in the morning. Of course all that order did was force the men to find a place to sleep for the night and there Sagamioska (or Sagami-Otsuka) was to serve the purpose.

The bars were like a little home away from home. You would get to know almost everyone in a very short time there was only about 250 souls in Sagami. It was a lot of fun to bum around from place to place teasing the JoSans and joking with them in half English half Japanese communication.

The Japanese language was not a easy one to learn. There were old words that were different then the new words. Also the Japanese had trouble pronouncing the R sound there was no sound like that in their language. It was shake wattle and wole, but learned some of their words and they learned some of ours. Basically we spoke in a mixture of the two such as "never hatcee" meaning never happen.

The bars probably had nice Japanese names when the kamikaze pilots frequented the place and the momasans who ran the places probably were JoSans at that time. Now since the Navy came to town they had names like The Texas, The Missouri, and The California.

We had Japanese men as gate guards they were from near by villages and were given special uniforms and allowed to carry a shot gun. This was a big privilege because after the war the Japanese were not allowed to have fire arms. The guards were allowed to take the guns home and they would go out bird hunting to help feed their families. They thought this was a wonderful present and were very proud gate guards and very efficient. I am sure there were a lot of guys looking for that job.

One day a gal I knew from Sagomi talked me into "catching a house" so I paid the mamasan about $20 and she was free. We found a nice one bedroom place on a farm not far from the base. The rent was $5 a month so it wasn't very expensive and this was completely furnished. I also now had a built in guide to take me around to see the country.

One weekend Cheasico took me and two of my crew mates on a trip to Kamakura, it was about twenty miles from the base. This town is on of the most religious places in Japan with two of the greatest shrines the Great Buddha and the magnificent Shinto Shrine.

First we went to the Great Buddha this is the largest cast bronze Buddha in the world. It was magnificent and we all took pictures standing in front of it. Then after some shopping we went over to the Shinto Shrine. You can always tell a Shinto Shrine because of the large wooden gateway consisting of two columns with a curve wooden section across the top, this was called the Torii Gate. The grounds were beautiful with a small lake where people could paddle small boats. There was a bridge of stone the surface was round and smooth it took all our effort to walk over it. The Shinto religion believed if a pregnant women walked across without falling then she would have a boy, if she fell she would probably have a miscarriage. We climbed up a long set of stone stairs lined with worshipers and at the top were the priest quarters and there was a curved piece of cloth about 20 feet wide where the people first would tie a prayer paper to a tree on each side of the barrier, then throw money into the curved pieces of cloth, bow, clap three times and walk away hoping that their prayers would be answered.

We went over to a small island just off the coast. The island was steep covered with pine trees and had only one way to get on the island. There were two stone lions guarding a swaying rope bridge onto the island. I am not sure what religious group this was but they worshiped nature. Now it was back to the farm where we lived. Cheasico was a great help I learned a lot of Japanese and got in touch with the local food. My favorite was fried rice it is nothing like we get in the United States with lots of vegetables and fish. We were not suppose to eat off the base because farmers used human fertilizer, where on the base organic fertilizer was used, they told us we would get sick if we ate the local food, but it never bothered me.

Boy did their vegetables grow big you would see a man carrying one carrot over his shoulder the size of a baseball bat.

The benjo which the toilet in Japan was called "doko desu benjo" where is the toilet. In the small towns there would be a door on the side of the house and the farmers would pay to clean it out, shoveling the shit into large wooden buckets. We called them honey bucket, and a cart pulled by a steer called a honey cart.

The farmers would put this in a pit on their farm and let it sit before putting it on the crops. One of our crew members was late for a flight and cut across a farm field to save time. He fell into one of those pits and he was a mess his legs swelled putting him in the hospital.

Back at the farm where we lived the farmers had two of the largest pigs I have ever seen. They were very proud of them and I took a picture of them smiling with their pigs it made them very happy.

When it was time to head back to Hawaii I paid the rent for four months, said goodbye and sadly left Fujisan (as the Japanese called it) never to see Cheasico again.

CHAPTER 11
BACK TO HAWAII,
THEN HOME ON LEAVE

Our 3 months in Japan were up and we were ready to return to Hawaii for the next six months.

Because we flew non stop to Hawaii and because we had bunks and home cooked food, a flight back in our plane was a luxury and every officer in Japan who had to return to Hawaii knew this. So they all decided to fly back on VW-1. So where will room for these officers be found in our plane? All the low ranking enlisted men were kicked off their own plane to make room for them and the remaining crew had to fly back short handed.

The only way for the seven crew men who were dropped off their plane to get back to Hawaii was to fly back MATS (Military Air Transport Service) and Island hop back in the old DC-3's. This was the old second World War two engine Douglas planes that were kindly called GOONEY BIRDS. I was mad and decided I better study and pass the test for the AT-2 (Aviation Electronic Technician Second Class), and also go to Escape and Evasion school in order to get my air crewman's wings. I won't island hop back to Hawaii the next time! There's no way I'm not going back with my plane next time.

I walked around my plane for the last time before they took off. There was hardly any room to walk because of all the things being brought back to Hawaii including two bicycles crowding the walk way. Ninety percent of all the junk belonged to the officers that kicked us off our plane. I hope that they didn't enjoy the flight, and that they would tell all their buddies not to take the ride from VW-1.

I watched my plane take off and had to wait three days for a seat on a MATS plane.

Here I was sitting in a bucket seat facing more bucket seats across the plane lined up facing each other. Not the most comfortable way to travel. The only good that came out of this trip was that we landed on

Wake Island and I could add another rock to my Island collection.

One of the islands I would have loved to land on was Hong Kong but we couldn't land there because as we were told, to land our plane we would have to have to fly over Chinese territory and if we got shot down, they could get a hold of all our sophisticated equipment. Looking back now, all I can say is "What a Joke," as you will find out later in this story.

As soon as I got back to Barbers Point, I was told that I had accrued too much leave time and that I should use some of my time up. The Navy had a sneaky way for you to get back to the States to take leave.

They sent me to a two week radio repair school at North Island Naval Base in San Diego, and then when the school was finished, I could take a 30 day leave.

So off I went - first to Ford Island at Pearl Harbor for transfer. And of course, for the few days I was there, while my paperwork was being processed, there was the beloved "shit duty." I think this is just a way to get things done around a base without using their own personnel. It's like a form of short term slavery, here was another reason to get a higher rank.

The first morning I stood in line with all the other enlisted men who were waiting for transfer. A

Chief Petty Officer walked along assigning jobs to each of us for the day. When he got to me, he handed me a lawn mower and said "Cut the grass." It had rained hard the night before (like only it can rain in Hawaii). There was standing water everywhere. "It's too wet to cut the grass," I complained. "Cut the grass" came back the answer. I took the lawn mower and ran it through a few mud puddles, got it real mucky and brought it back. "See I told you it was too wet to cut the grass", I said. "Then water it," he replied. I looked at the chief startled in disbelief. "On the days we don't cut the grass, we water, orders are orders," he replied. At this point, I thought of an old Navy saying, there is the right way and then there is the Navy way. I took the hose and sprinkler, set it up in a puddle and dared anyone to prove I didn't water the grass. I then went and drank coffee all morning.

The strange thing about all of this was that I was sent right back to Barbers Point to catch a plane, it was just a waste of a few days.

The school at North Island was a joke. I didn't learn anything that I didn't already know, but at least it was a way for me to get home on leave for awhile.

When the school was finished, another sailor and I caught a hop to San Antonio. It was the only one going that day, so we took it.

At the Air Force Base in San Antonio, there were no hops going out, and they said we could have better luck in Houston. One of the airmen gave us a ride out of town to a spot where he said we could catch a ride. It was getting dark and there was one street light and a closed gas station. We spent half the night dropping rocks on large roaches that were crossing the roadway.

In the early morning, a car stopped and offered us a ride. There were two black Air Force guys in the car. They told us "we picked you up because we need you in case we have car trouble. Texas is not kind to stranded black folks".

They drove us to the Houston Air Force Base. My partner got a plane right away, but I had to stay overnight in a transit dorm. I got a call early in the morning. "A jeep will pick you up in ten minutes, we have a hop for you," the voice said.

When I got to the air strip, there was a B-15 Billy Mitchell two engine bomber waiting. I was stuck in a tight spot, behind the bomb bay where the tail gunner used to sit, there was one small window, but at least it was a ride.

The bomb bay was loaded with cases of rum and the plane had just flown up from Cuba and was headed to Omaha. I guess you could call them Rum Runners.

At Omaha, there were no more flights going my way, so one of the airmen who were just getting off duty took me out of town to the Iowa side of the river so I could catch a ride. A salesman was going to Des Moines said, "Hop in," and I was on my way again. In those days, the only people hitchhiking were service men. So it was always easy to get a ride and I put a lot of crazy miles on my thumb.

One time in L.A., two good looking girls picked me up and brought me to one of their homes. Then the phone rang and one of the girl's mothers ordered her home. So there I was, back on the same corner 15 minutes later.

Another time, in Salt Lake City, I was thumbing with another sailor and a car with four gals picked us up. We bar hopped in all kinds of crazy places in the mountains. We did a lot of dancing and four hours later, my friend went home with one of the girls. I picked the wrong one to pay attention to and I was once again back on the same corner I started from.

When we got to Des Moines, the salesman said you can't go through town without stopping at Sally's Place. So he took me there. The bar was owned and operated by Sally. She was a retired stripper and she would sing and dance for the customers. Then for a special customer, she would come over to the table, balance a glass on her 50 D's and pour beer into it and then did the same with the other glass. This was quite a place.

The salesman dropped me off on the road to Minneapolis. I waited there about five minutes when a car loaded with football fans picked me up. They were going to a game against the Minnesota Gophers the next day. They dropped me off on the north side of Minneapolis. It was about midnight and two women, probably in their mid 30's, picked me up. They were drunk and still wanted to party and talked me into going along to one of their houses, but then, one of them got real sick and they said "sorry," and I was back on the highway with my thumb out. Three more rides and I made it home in the morning.

My stay at home was uneventful and before I knew it, my leave was up and I had to head back. My parents drove me to a highway leading out west of Minneapolis, after I checked and found no hops heading west at the local Air Force facility.

Now days I marvel at my parents having the trust in me to drop me off on a corner so I could hitchhike 2000 miles. Of course things were different 50 years ago. Later I found out that mom and dad stayed out of my site, and kept a eye on me until I got a ride.

I guess they were use to me thumbing a ride. Lenny and I would bum a ride over to Virginia, a near by town 25 miles away, and attend the teenage dances. We liked going over there, because we knew more kids on a personal level then even in our own town, and because of this guys would give us a ride over there so we could introduce them to the girls.

One winter evening four of us in Sweed Erickson's old car picked up two girls that Lenny and I knew, and we road around town for a while. Sweed said that because it was his car Lenny and I should go and buy some beer. As under age kids we were able to buy beer in a small grocery store across the street from the police station because the owner knew us. We got out of the car, it was bitter cold out, probably ten degrees below zero. Lenny was wearing one of the girls woolen cap and mittens. When we entered the store, Sweed drove away with the girls leaving us stranded miles from home without a hat or gloves. There we were standing back to back with the girls woolen cap stretched over both our heads and one mitten each hitchhiking home. Needless to say it was a freezing experience.

A guy came along after my parents dropped me off needed help driving, and we had it to Frisco in short order driving day and night. Three days at Treasure Island and a quick plane ride and Hawaii here I come!!

CHAPTER 12
ESCAPE & EVASION
SCHOOL

When I got back to Barbers Point, I found out my old Buick had bit the dust. I needed to find a new junker to get me around. There were always cars to be picked up cheap. If you were transferred back to the U.S., were not a First Class or above, or the car was less than 5 years old, or if you owed money on the car, the government would not ship it back for you. A lot of times there would be a car even a very nice old one available. Like one time there was a fairly new MG sitting there with all the papers on the front seat and a sign saying, "just take over the payments."

I found a cheap car; it was a light blue 1940 Ford two door, it suited my purpose and I could just leave it when I went back to get discharged. It was August, 1955, and in 10 months I get to go home, but first there was Escape & Evasion school and another trip to Japan in February.

I wanted to get my Air Crewmen wings and designation. One of the requirements was Escape & Evasion School which was run by the Army out of Scofield Barracks. You remember Scofield, it was in the center of the island and the place the movie, *From Here to Eternity* was about.

There were 20 men in a class and we were given flight suits to put on showing no ranking. Here we were men from different squadrons and about half were officers.

We were bussed up to the North West corner of Oahu called Kaena Point. There was an old base in the area and it was government land. It was a desolate uninhabited area with old dirt trails running through it.

In the morning, they drove us down a dirt road in the bed of an old dump truck. They told us that we were ten miles from the ocean and we would have to make our way across the swamps and hills to the coast. There we would be sent out in rubber rafts and picked up by helicopters. This was to teach us how to get through enemy territory and how to get rescued from the sea if we got shot down.

Also, all through the ten miles there would be Chinese Communist soldiers scattered about. These, of course, would be Army soldiers playing the part. If we got captured, we would be taken to a prison camp.

They would drop us off the dump truck two at a time every one hundred yards apart and gave us a compass as our only tool and said good luck.

My partner and I (his name was Joe) jumped into the underbrush and started crawling through the muck and mud over hills and back into the slop.

The droppings we came across looked like they belonged to wild pigs. Luckily there were no snakes on Oahu. Hawaii had Mongoose and they cleaned them all out. Or atleast that was what we were told.

We tried to stay in the low bad areas. We figured that the enemy would not want to get dirty. After traveling for many hours, we came across another dirt trail. We saw some enemy soldiers, so we remained hidden. After a while, they got busy capturing some guys up the road and so seeing that the coast was clear, we scurried across the road and hid on the other side. We were in the brush when all of a sudden; more enemy soldiers come by and stopped right where we were hidden. They were so close; I could count the laces on their boots. We held our breath. It was a hot day and sweat was dripping off my face. I was afraid a droplet would hit a leaf and give us away. After a while, they moved away from our position and I said, "Let's go!"

Another three hours of crawling we did not see any enemy in site. We figured that they stationed themselves along the path and caught most of the guys trying to cross. Why get dirty crawling through the brush, they weren't that dumb.

We made it through to the ocean and two other groups were there; six out of twenty had made it through. There were no life rafts, no helicopters, like we were told. They lied to us. They told us we had done a great job getting through the trial and now we would be brought back to camp where we would get a hot meal, a hot shower, a change of clothes, and a bunk for the night. This sounded great, because I hadn't eaten all day, it was supper time and I was dead tired.

We were told to just follow the trail that was on our left and we only had to walk about a half mile to camp. As were walking up a hill, all of a sudden, three communist soldiers with rifles jumped up and captured us. We were marched to an area where there was a building and a barbed wire compound, and in that area were all the rest of the twenty that started out. We were lied to again. We were placed in the compound along with the other men.

Everything seemed real and everyone went along with it. We were tired, hungry and everything that had happened had be a psychological scheme to make us feel like it was really happening. I could have stood up and said, "I Quit," and nothing would have happed except you would have flunked the school and there would be no crewman designation. It felt real and you believed what was happening.

They spoke and dressed like Chinese soldiers or at least something that sounded like Chinese. This helped with the illusion and you really hated them. They would torment us. Pour water on the ground, we hadn't had a drink all day and here it was evening and getting dark out.

If you got close to the wire, they would take a stick and trip you or push you down with the butt of their rifles. They would make you duck walk in a row around the area. If you didn't say "Quack" as you walked, they would push you over and laugh at you.

And then they would take a guy away when they were ready to collapse or who fell down and were unable to move. Our group kept getting smaller as night approached.

I kept thinking you can't break me I will keep going, this has to stop sometime. Finally I keeled over on the barbed wire and they hauled me out. I was sat down in the dark in front of a desk with a bright hot light in my face. A man, who spoke in bad English, started to ask me questions. They asked me many questions; like do you like your mother? "I said yes". Do you like Chinese Communists? "I said no." Then they played it back. Do you like your mother? "no". Do you like China? "yes," they had switched answers on me.

Then it was over. I was admonished for saying yes and no. Only your name, rank and service number I was told to say.

I was then given a piece of canvas and a K ration and told to go out in back and find a piece of ground to sleep on. I was so tired that I could have slept standing up. Sleep came very easy that night.

On the bus trip back, some of the guys said that if they ever met one of these Army guys in town, their life wouldn't be worth a nickel.

I never saw one of them again. I think they were there for maybe six months and then shipped out to save their lives.

We spent our time the next few months, mostly skin diving. Just off our base, was Nimitz Beach. We would take a rubber raft and paddle out a few hundred yards and tie up to the propeller of a sunken Corsair from the second World War and go fishing. I had a double rubber spear gun and we always caught fish. We caught most red snapper and a few lobsters. These were the spiney kind, no claws, like the ones from the Atlantic. We would grab them as they tried to scurry back to their holes.

In all my hours of swimming, I never saw a shark, but we were always watchful for them. Moray Eels were the bad guys around when we were swimming. There was a colony of them living down in the sunken plane. It was said that if you shot one, they would climb right up your spear and attack.

Two of us decided to catch a Moray Eel. We had to coordinate our attack and fire at the same time, one shot in the head and one shot in the tail. We saw one sticking out from below the plane. John shot the head and as he pulled it out, I got it in the tail. We stretched him between us and brought it to shore for pictures. It was still snapping when we got it up the beach.

Catch of the Day

Another time we drove up the where the road ends on the west side of the Island. We decided to go on a shark hunt, so we took a large hook with a bloody piece of meat and took it out in the ocean about 100 yards. We got the beer out and hot dogs and started to build a bond fire. The wood was a little damp, so smart me, decided to siphon a little gas in a beer can. By the time I got back to the group, the fire was going, so taking a precaution; I stood about 10 feet away and threw the gas on the fire. To my amazement, the fire climbed back up the stream of gas instantly and the can in my hand went pop! I wasn't hurt but I learned a big lesson. Needless to say, we never caught a shark but it still was a good time for us all.

CHAPTER 13
BACK TO JAPAN

The 6 months flew by it was February 1956 and we were headed back to Atsugi. Everyone was in high spirits. Back to Babysan, funny money, cheap beer, and the crazy mixed up language of part English and part Japanese.

Speaking of language, we would ask a Momasan "what is hot water" in Japanese. (Oh you) was the reply. "What is the morning" (kissa) was the reply. "Every morning" in old Japanese (My assa). This would generate a big laugh and usually a free beer. Momasan would say "You very smart GI."

Speaking of Babysan or Joesan, most Japanese girls were beautiful, very seldom have I seen an ugly girl. They were very smart and always want to please a guy. Many of the GI's would have married their girlfriends, but the government would not allow it when I was there. We would have a lot of fun with them in the bars. They loved playing little games and always had a tremendous sense of joy and laughter. If it sounds like I was enthralled with Babysan, I think all the servicemen were.

As far as cheap beer is concerned, it was Nippon or Kerren at 500 yen or $1.40 a quart. The money we used off the base in Japan was the yen.

There was 360 yen to the dollar. Of course, there were no dollars or green backs as we know them. The Government did not want our money getting into foreign hands, so we were paid in script. Officially called Military Payment Certificates – little paper money which we called funny money. It ranged from a 5 cent bill to 20 dollars.

We would then change the script at the bank on the base to whatever currency was at the place we were at.

In Okinawa, we used "B Yen", Military Currency issued by our government because Okinawa was our protectorate and we ran the island for many years before giving it back to Japan.

Crew Patch

In the Philippines, their money was issued by their Central Bank and was valued at ½ US.

Flying back to Japan, you cross the International Date Line, so you lose a day going and coming back you land in Hawaii before you left Japan. This time we didn't stop at Guam, but flew nonstop all the way to Atsugi. Everything looked the same – I was glad to be back. Even the smell was there, Japan had a distinct order all its own.

It was early in February, no snow but cold and damp. When the sun was out, it was nice, but the nights were wicked. We were lucky we had leather flight jackets issued to us for use, not to keep. We brought civilian cloth to wear when not on duty, and with the Hong Kong tailor shop on the base we always left with more than we came with. I had a beautiful camel hair coat made that I cherished for many years and then it kept some homeless person warm for years after that.

The first chance I had after landing and storing my gear was a trip into Sagami. It still looked the same. I saw some of the familiar Josan's around and I checked in where Chiesgco had been working. She was not around and the didn't know what had happened to her. "The last time we saw her she left with you," was the reply. I stopped in the bar Lone Star (our squadron hang out), but it was a quiet day. I then went over to the Missouri to joke with the gals. Peanuts said, "Olysaun, where have you been? No see you long time." "Hawaii," I said, "but I will be around now for a long time," I told her. Then it was back to the base before the gate closed and I would have to find a Josan to share a bed with.

The Josan's or Babysan, as the GI's called them, were unique to Japan and with our small town of

Sagamioska, I think we had the best situation in the country. Josan had won the serviceman's affection and made their stay in this strange land a pleasant and unforgettable one. I still have fond memories of my time there in the land of Fugesan. I still can say many phrases in their language – like dai-jobu (means OK). In a thousand ways, our occupation changed the way the young people think and I feel the vast modern country it has become had a lot to do with the GI's being there. We fell in love with the country and they fell in love with the U.S.

As I wandered back to the base that day, I wondered if I would ever find that certain Josan that would light up my life. I guess I'll just have to keep on looking.

CHAPTER 14
TRIP TO IWO JIMA

We barely were settled in Japan, when off to Iwo Jima we flew. I never knew the reason we went there, but then most of the time they never told us the reason. I had to scratch my head on this one because only the plane crew came along – we didn't take our radar passengers. The plan was that we would be there three days.

The base was an Air Force Base. I will say without a doubt that they had some of the worst duty stations. I know the Navy had some too, but Iwo Jima had to be the worst in the whole armed forces.

Because of the windy conditions and the fact that most pacific storms seem to go across Iwo Jima, the personnel lived in tents. The only real buildings were the offices, the chow hall, the officer's housing and the service clubs. They showed movies on the back side of one of the few stationary structures.

Mount Serabachi

Mount Serabachi

After seeing the smelly tent assigned to us, we decided to live on our plane. There were 8 enlisted men and 8 bunks so everything was perfect.

Also, because the supply boat was late in coming, food was scarce, so we ate on our plane. There was no beer in the enlisted men's' club, but the officers club had hard liquor.

So we took off our white hats and in flight suits we all looked the same (no ranks were shown on enlisted men's flight suits). So you couldn't tell us apart from our officers. So we went to their club and drank their booze.

If the enlisted men on this island were good and didn't cause trouble, they could go to Tokyo for a week. To me, Tokyo wasn't a great liberty town. It was like Yokohama – all full of buy me a drink clubs or taxi dance joints. What a lousy duty station. They didn't even have movies because the supply ship was late.

The next day we borrowed a truck and driver and went sight seeing around the island.   From the air, Iwo looked like a fat exclamation mark with Mount Serabachi, the dot on the end. Serabachi was an extinct volcano and when it erupted a century or so ago, it formed the island and the whole place is all black volcano sand.

The Marines officially took Iwo Jima on march 26, 1945, after a 31 day battle that pitted some 100,000 U. S. troops against 21,200 Japanese. Some 6,821 Americans were killed, only 1,033 Japanese survived.

There were native inhabitants on the island, but the Japanese kicked them out when they wanted to use the island for a strategic base. Now days the original inhabitants and there descendants want to return, but the Japanese Government has said that it was too dangerous because they are still finding live ammunition, and human remains, and the caves have still not been cleaned out.

First, we drove down to the beach to see where the Marines landed. We had to stop driving our truck on the black beach because we started to sink down in the sand. We stepped down from the truck and sunk a few inches in the stuff. There were many rusting landing barges on the shore. They would all rust down to nothing and go back to nature.

After a few hundred feet of this soft volcanic sand, came a short cliff, about 20 or 30 feet high. There were caves dug into the cliff and concrete pill boxes crumbling on top. The caves were open with large signs saying DO NOT ENTER LIVE AMMUNITION AND DEAD JAPANESE INSIDE.

The concrete gun emplacements were all blown up, but one could tell what originally was there.

The center of the island was a large flat plateau with the air strip on it. That was the reason for taking the island during the Second World War. The air strip gave us a platform to bomb Japan from.

There was the mountain with the Japanese firing down on anything that moved. How the Marines landed and took this island is beyond my imagination. We drove up to the top of Mount Seriboshi. It's a desolate hill with no place to hide and the enemy shooting down on our troops, it was hell to take the hill. At the top there was a white monument with an American flag flying. They must put the flag up every morning and take it down every night. This is the same location where the original flag was raised in that famous picture.

We drove to the bottom side of the island and in the side of a hill, someone had carved a portrait of the famous flag raising and then white washed it.

We laid around on the air strip for the remaining three days. I was never so glad to get away from the place.

Now it was back to Japan and the terrible duty in Atsugi and Sagami. The problem was that being back for a week we had another mission

CHAPTER 15
FLIGHT TO OKINAWA

This time we landed on another Air Force Base at Naha, Okinawa. The Base was just outside of the capital and largest city of Naha. The island was a US Protectorate since the Second World War, and that meant that the U.S. ran the island and even supplied them with a U.S. version of the Yen to be used for money. The dreaded B Yen. We called it dreaded because in Japan you could exchange Yen back into script, but in Okinawa, you couldn't. So, if you left the island and weren't careful, you could end up with a pocketful of useless B Yen. I know, because I still have some 50 years later.

Naha was near the southern tip of the island and the base was near the coast. From there in fact, the base was near when the Marines landed and there were rusting landing barges in the surf. It seems that everywhere we go there is rusting remnants of the Second World War. You could tear off a two inch piece of steel and just crumble it in your hand. Maybe that was the idea as soon they would crumble into nothing.

Our detachment was at the south end of the base. There were barracks and a chow hall and the Hobeau Haven, our recreation and beer hall. The beer was Tigre beer from Singapore.

The word Hobeau was a native word for cobra, which the island was crawling with. The crew would find long sticks and carve them up to individualize them. When you walked down a path, you would move the stick from side to side to keep the cobra at bay. To tell the truth, we never saw one in the wild.

The food was great, we just had to ask for the raw ingredients and the Air Force supplied our needs. The detachment was small, they never missed our small amount, so we ate a lot of steak.

First order of the day, once we got settled in, was to go and visit Naha. We took a bus from the base to town. The simplest way to describe Naha was it stunk. The rickety shops were along the road and a river ran behind and this was their open sewer. I took a picture of it and worried if I got caught taking the picture. There were a few brand new buildings, one was the bank; the other was a government building. There were street vendors advertising Hobeau Mongoose fights. We paid to watch one and that was enough. The cobra would sit up and hiss and the Mongoose paid no attention to the snake. All of a sudden, the cobra struck. The Mongoose lightning quick moved out of the way, then grabbed the snake by the neck and that was the end of the snake. You saw one, you saw them all because the Mongoose never lost!

The only interesting thing that happened that day was there was a model agency along the road with a sign saying, "take pictures of totally naked beauties." Of course it was for a price. What made this interesting was in Japan, it would never happen, no one could take pictures with no clothes on the Japanese girls were very shy and didn't run around naked.

I had the camera and two of the guys with me, paid to watch. I took a role of color slides and still have them to this day. It was my one and only trip to town. I bought nothing, drank nothing, was hungry, but was back to base for supper.

Later we were told that staying in town after dark was dangerous. The only way back to the base at night was by taxi and they weren't to be trusted.

Being in Okinawa wasn't so bad we had good food and were flying almost every day.

The reason we were in Naha was never made clear at the time. However we would find out later what it was all about. We were the only plane from VW-1 on the base we would be there for two weeks and then another plane would take our place.

We would fly down to Hong Kong and then up the Chinese coast twenty-four miles out. 12 miles is the normal territory limits of a country around the world, but the Chinese said they would shoot down any plane that came within 20 miles of their territory and that included islands. We would fly along the coast to Shanghai and then turn away and return to Naha. These flights would take place almost every day and our squadron had been doing this for a few months. We even had a Chinese Mig fly out and check us over he could have shot us down real easy. One time we stood radar watch while the Navy sent a Phantom aerial photo plane into China to take photos of their installations and hurry out while we stood watch for MIGS.

Woom Toom

We had to be real careful to stay away from their islands. In 2001 a Navy radar plane got too close to one of their islands and a MIG crashed into it, causing it to crash land on one of their islands. Some of our men lost their lives. The Chinese got a hold of the plane and all its secret equipment. There was quite a haggle to get our men and the plane back, so you see what we were doing could have been dangerous. We didn't know it at the time, but the Chinese were being set up.

We had heard of the womb tombs that were unique to Okinawa. So three of us decided to go out one day when we were not flying and look for them in the countryside. They were scattered around and one could be spotted because the farmers would plow around them. So if you saw a large clump of bushes in the middle of a plowed field you could bet it was a tomb. They were built many hundreds of years ago and were considered sacred by the natives and not to be touched.

So camera in hand and with our trusty hobeau sticks, the three of us went looking for them. There was a concrete dome about 15 feet square. It even had a belly button in the middle. There were two ornate legs and a stone covered entrance between the legs. Their belief was that where you came from back you go.

Well our time was up on Okinawa now, back to good old Fujisan and the Josans.

Chapter 16
Sagamioska

We were finally back in Atsugi. Since we got here we have been gone most of the time, first to Ewo and then to Naha. We have been in Japan for three weeks and I spent part of one day roaming around Sagami.

It was the early part of March, 1956, still winter time in Japan. Cool in the daylight but bitter cold at night. No snow except on the mountain tops, but with the high humidity the cold went right through you, and we found good use for our flight jackets.

In the little bars in Sagamioska there would be a hibachi pot sitting in a three foot square sand enclosure. This was a large iron pot that they would burn charcoal in. This was the only source of heat, so everyone huddled near the hibachi.

All the bars were very similar to each other. There would be a small bar with two or three stools and Momasan behind the bar running everything. The main room was about 25 foot square with three small tables and chairs and usually there would be three girls or Jo Sans as hostesses. Of course there were a few larger bars with double the amount of everything. And then there was the Fuji, a large two story building that was all by itself across the train tracks. Our theory was that this was built for the Japanese officers while the rest of the town was for the pilots that were trained to die for the Emperor.

Next to the bar usually was a shoji screen and when you walked around the screen there was a hallway running back about 20 feet with a binjo (toilet) on the left, no door, just a highly polished floor with a 18 inch square hole in the middle of it and a wood cover over it. They would squat over the hole and let it fly. Continuing on, there was a large wooden tub filled with water with a hibachi heating it from below. Everyone staying the night would climb in, boys, girls, and mamasan, you couldn't go to bed dirty. One of my crew mates was telling about the hotsi bath when he was drunk, and he said," there were boobies here and boobies there, boobies floating everywhere."

Down the hall across from the binjo were four bedrooms for each josan and momasan.

Before taking a hotsibath, the josan would take charcoal from the hibachi pot, put it in a metal pan with a cover and long handle and slip it under the covers of her bed. The pan in the bed was not the total answer. It took a lot of covers and body heat to keep warm and running to the binjo in the middle of the night was a freezing experience.

As I stated, there was no door on the binjo and all toilets in Japan that I saw were unisex. It was nothing to be standing at a urinal in a big Yokahama department store and have a woman walk by and go into a toilet stall.

Sagimioska was the most unique place in all of Japan and probably the world. Because Atsugi was the Kamikaze pilot's base, and sagami was built for them, it was where they enjoyed themselves with wine, women and song before killing themselves. Nothing had changed in 10 years following the war except the names of the bars. I shouldn't call them bars, because you could get a bite to eat and enjoy the Josans and for staying the night, it was strictly up to you. Another name could be a home away from home. No flashing lights, but now the names were Americanized and many were named after states.

I never saw an officer on the streets of Sagami. I don't know where they went for liberty. I saw very few Japanese men around, but then so many got killed in the war that there weren't that many left.

First night in Sagami, it's always the same. There's sixty-one bars in its Hall of Fame. There's Josan a plenty – just made for you. All you need is the Yen - 1500 will do.

This was our town and the squadrons permanently stationed there took turns pulling shore patrol. I had the Shore Patrol duty twice. So we knew the town and were on speaking terms with most of the Josans.

When aircraft carriers would visit Youkuska (a large naval base 30 miles south of Atsugi), the planes would land at Atsugi. We called these men, "Ship Board Sailors." We didn't like it when they came over and the Shore Patrol would make it rough on them. There were about 20 bars we would send them to – we called these Ship Board Bars and they were all lined up on the main street and were not places where us locals would visit. Also, we would send them to Yokahama, bragging up what a wonderful place it was. No Ship Board Sailor was going to run our town. Each squadron had their own hang out. Ours was the Bar Lone Star it was a large bar with about six Josan working there. I didn't care for the place that much, so I would stop in, say hi and be on my way.

One of the bars I liked to visit was the Missouri. It was up the street on the way out of town and it was a large place like the bar Lone Star. All the girls were always playing silly games and laughing was the most common thing spoken. It was a fun place to visit. and spend some time, but I never stayed there. The girls were a fun loving lot and their ring leader was Peanuts. She was called that because guys would toss peanuts in the air and she would catch them in her mouth. She would always tease me about not staying there. I would say that I was having too much fun and laughing too hard to fall in love. "Maybe you have a sweetheart somewhere else," they would say.

So this was Sagami. There was no need to go to Yokahama, but a trip there was looming on the horizon.

CHAPTER 17
GOING TO YOKOHAMA

Yokahama was Japan's second largest city and I was surprised to see that it was still showing ravishes of the war, but there was a large industrial complex that was ripe for bombing and it still showed.

Shopping was the main reason for me going there. The shops were interesting and you had to barter for everything, in fact, I don't think they would sell it to you if you didn't barter. I would hold up an item and say "How much you speak." They would give a price which I would cut in half and then we would go back and forth and meet somewhere in the middle and everyone was happy. I still paid too much for the item and they made a profit, but with prices so low and dealing with 360 yen to the dollar, we really made out.

I planned to go to college and study architecture when I got out, so I bought a good slide rule and some wonderful drafting tools.   I also bought two good cameras, a Minolta single lens, and a Yashickaflex Reflex.   All the items I still have and buying a camera over there was a no brainer because of the great lenses they made.

Getting there was no problem.   Yokahama was only a short distance from the base, and the trains were fast and cheap, and it took just a short time to get there.   On the train, many of the people wore masks. In such a small over populated country no one wanted to spread germs.   Otherwise, they seemed to always be reading something.

On one of my trips, the train stopped at a small station and there was another train going the other way.   I looked across and there was Cheasico with a couple of girlfriends.   I waved to her and she gave me a startled look and pointed and then the train departed.   At least I know nothing had happened to my former housemate; that was the only time I ever saw her.

Another way to go to town was by Taxi.   There were small boxy cars and they had little arms that would flip out from the door post for a turn signal. It was beep, beep and go as far as they could with pedestrians jumping out of the way. It was like riding in go carts at the fairgrounds. The taxis were the only cars on the street. There were also a lot of bicycles, motorcycles, and there even was a motorcycle pick-up. No Hondas or Toyotas around, but with the great train service, who needed a car.

Most of the bars were taxi dancing places, where you bought a ticket and you could dance or sit with the Josan; one ticket per length of the dance.

Other bars were "buy me a drink" places. Where as soon as you entered a Josan would latch onto you and of course, "buy me a drink" they would say. The sailor would fall for their sweet talk and buy them an expensive drink, usually consisting of tea, looking like a cocktail. Needless to say, I got out of these places as soon as I could.

In the taxi dance places you could sit up at the bar and you wouldn't be bothered. So in Yokahama, when I wanted a beer, that's where I went.

I was sitting at the end of the bar and the cashier was just a few feet away selling dance tickets. I struck up a conversation with her. She was about five years older than me, and spoke perfect English and of course was very pretty as all Japanese Josans seemed to be. We talked for a long time and I had three or four beers and was feeling my oats. When the bar was about ready to close, she asked me to go home with her and of course I said "Di jobi" yes.

We got in a taxi and she rattled off where to go and after a long ride, we ended up in an old neighborhood of traditional Japanese homes. We got out of the cab a few blocks from her house and walked quietly up the street with her putting a finger to her mouth, telling me to be quiet. The homes looked like you would see in an old movie. She slid a shoji screen aside (this is a wooden sliding screen with thin wooden mullions and glazed with rice paper).

Inside the floor was covered with tatami mats (these are mats made from rice straw with a black edge). It could take many mats to cover a room and all rooms were sized to fit the mats. There were sliding shoji screens everywhere and we tiptoed through one of them to what was her room. We had to be quiet because her parents slept near by and shoji screens did not keep out the sound. There were candles in jars around for light. She rolled out a sleeping mat and said doso (please).

It turned out to be not such a great night because we had to be so quiet. Before sunrise, I had to get up and quietly leave. She walked me to a corner where she said taxis passed by all the time and we said goodbye. I felt so guilty for taking advantage of her. I never went back to the bar where she worked and never saw her again.

Another interesting time in Yokahama was when many members of our squadron bought lots of suits and coats from the Hong Kong tailors located on the base. I bought a camelhair overcoat and two suits, and because our squadron was such a good customer, they gave us a party at a special Chinese restaurant. We were brought in Taxies to a large party room. It was a twenty course meal with everything imaginable. There were two large triple decker lazy susan covered with all the food. One of the things that they had, stuck in my mind these many years were called blutes (these were called 100 year old eggs). The Chinese bury eggs and then dig up there great grandfather's eggs, it's a continuing process. They were a beautiful shade of green with a dark green yoke. I was a little squeamish to taste one at first, but they tasted ok.

After we had stuffed ourselves with all the wonderful food, they taxied us back to the base. This meal was one of my fondest memory of Yokahama.

Peanuts

Acami

CHAPTER 18
MEETING ACAMI

One night I stopped in the Missouri Bar, I had been wandering around Sagami and I stopped into the bar Lonestar, but it was quiet and there was no one around I knew to talk to. The Missouri Bar was always fun to stop by, because It was always a happy place with the gal called Peanuts as the ring leader. Peanuts came over as soon as I entered the bar and said, "Oliesan I have a girl for you, because you don't have a steady girlfriend." "Who do you suggest" I said looking at Peanuts and the girls. "No" she said, "you not hot for us because you never stay here. There is a new girl who just came to Sagami yesterday and is beautiful, just meant for you," she replied. "Where is this wonder?" I asked. "The Club Oasis" she replied. "I don't believe you I have been all over Sagami and even pulled shore patrol, there is no such place," I replied. "Go down the alley next door and you will find it" she said. "Go down the alley and you will, It's not very pretty and hardly looks like a bar, but it's been here all the time," was the answer.

I headed down the dark dingy alley way and there it was. It was dimly lit, with a sign that was hard to read. "No wonder I never found it," I thought, "hardly anyone would have ever found this."

I walked in and it indeed was not very pleasant looking. Momasan was behind the bar she looked tired and old and there was no business. The place was clean but clearly not inviting. More like an original Kamikaze bar, more Japanese looking, less American. There were two very plain looking Josans sitting at the small tables and then the most beautiful Japanese girl I ever saw. She was perfectly dressed without a hair out of place. She looked like a Japanese doll in western style clothes. Her face did not have the typical Japanese look and I thought maybe she was Eurasian.

I walked over and asked her name. "I am Acami Inou" she replied in perfect English. I was surprised because I was used to the chip chop half Japanese, half American, that was the usual chatter.

I sat down, ordered a beer and asked her to sit with me. "I came from a Catholic orphanage on the island of Shikoku and also I am a Christian. When I turned 18, I had to leave and the Momasan found me. Acami Inou was the name they gave me at the orphanage" she said.

We talked for hours and I was smitten with this beautiful, intelligent woman. I told Momasan that I wouldn't stay the night, that I wanted our first encounter to blossom first. She said, "I understand." I told her that now that I know where the Oasis was, that I would bring my friends over. "Domo" she said and I left, that is thank you in Japanese. I thought as I walked down the street the other two girls are fair game but Acami is mine!

From that day on I spent every day and night with Acami. On my duty nights, I would pay for her time. Momasan was agreeable to this because I was bringing business to the Oasis.

I would pick her up and we would go to the EM Club on the base for super and dancing. The Enlisted Men's' Club had dance bands and floor shows on weekends. On my days off, we would take buying trips to Yokahama (I bought all my tools to use in my future architectural profession). Or we would play miniature golf on the base, or just go out picture taking in the countryside, and of course many pictures of Acami. She was a dream for a photographer, because she just couldn't take a bad picture. Of course there were never any no clothes pictures, but I took some very sexy ones.

I was madly in love and Acami's feelings were mutual. We talked about getting married. I went and talked to the base Chaplain and I was told that marrying a Japanese girl was not allowed. This tore me apart! I would have married her in a moment. She was everything I imagined a soul mate would be.

But again, Mrs. Roosevelt was against American Servicemen marrying Japanese girls when she visited Japan and talked to the Commander of the Pacific Fleet.

In hind sight, if we would have gotten married, as a twenty-one year old with no future in Civilian life, my only solution would have been to say in the service and spend my 20 years in the Navy. My whole life from this point on would have changed. It is interesting how one small change in the passing of time would send one's life in a total different direction.

But as long as I was in Japan, Acami and I would be together, and I dreaded the day when I would have to leave. I thought of what kind of children we could have had. They would have been beautiful, with a Swedish Japanese mixture, and with such a beautiful mother how could they go wrong.

As I put down my memories of Acami fifty years later, there is still such a soft spot in my heart for her. She was my first true love.

CHAPTER 19
A FLIGHT TO OBLIVIAN

It was just after lunch, and we were the duty plane. That meant that we had the duty, had to stay on the base and report where we were in case of any emergency. There were three planes in Japan at any one time, and so the duty came around every three days. Also we had to do all the odd jobs the squadron needed. On this day, I was driving a jeep around the base delivering messages.

Another plane was scheduled for a flight, but the crew was not on the base, so they couldn't be found. In retrospect, they did not want to go on the mission and their captain told them to get lost. I'm not sure how they knew what the mission was, but someone leaked the information.

Here we were the duty plane and had to be on base, so the mission fell to us. The crew was called in for a meeting while our plane was getting ready.

We were told that we will take a flight up the Chinese coast as usual. We will have a P-2V for protection (a P2-V was a pursuit bomber with two engines turning and two engines burning. In other words, they had jet pods and flew twice as fast as we flew). When we got to Shanghai, instead of turning away toward Okinawa, we were to fly into China over the city to the largest air base in the Orient and take radar pictures of the base. When necessary, cameras record automatically any pictures on the radarscope for further reference. We were told that if we got shot down or crashed, that we were to make our way to the coast to get picked up. In hindsight, we would have never made it to the coast with China's largest city standing in the way. This was a suicide mission – there would never have been anyone at the coast to pick us up if we actually made it to the coast. If we survived getting shot down a Chinese prison probably awaited us. I could just see eating wormy rice for the next twenty years, but at this time, it never entered my mind and I don't think it was foremost on the minds of our crew. They gave us sidearms (a 45), some Chinese money, and strips of Chinese writing that was supposed to ask for help. Who knows, it could have said shoot us on sight I jokingly thought. We were told that if you lay low near a farm house and the people would bow down in the morning and pray that they were Buddhists and they would not harm you, big deal no comfort there.

They had us get rid of all our personal information and then said good luck. We took off in the evening and the sun was going down. All our previous flights up the coast were conducted in the daylight. I hoped the Chinese didn't know the difference, ha, ha. All the flights up the Chinese coast were so they would get us to us we were setting them up for this flight.

As we took off and flew south out of Japan I passed the time pondering my life up to that time, not in a fatalistic way, but what have I achieved in life up to this time on earth. I have no wife, no children no one to leave a legacy to. I had accomplished nothing of importance in any possible way to further mankind. I thought back to the lonely little boy who because of his learning disabilities felt unacceptable to his peers. How the Navy had opened up his life, and he had come such a great distance in three years, and now was a crew member on a great aircraft about to fly into oblivion.

With the P-2V flying with us the trip down to Hong Kong was uneventful, but as we started up the coast we should have thought something was strange when the faster P-2V was 500 miles behind us. They know what was going on and didn't want to be nowhere near us when the MIGs came a calling. If we were attacked, our plane had no protection except the sidearms we were issued. I can just see us shooting down a MIG-16 with a 45.

This was the only time in the Navy that I had a pistol. I had never fired a 45 and didn't really know how to, and they didn't give us instructions when they handed them out. We fired old Springfield rifles in boot camp, and on Shore Patrol we only carried night sticks, and on post watches a rifle was issued to us.

As I sat at the radio desk I had nothing to do because it was radio silence. I had thoughts as I dreamed of a MIG flying at me and I would grab the flare gun hanging above the desk. I would shoot the flare at the plane and it would go right in the jet engine and the plane would blow up.

Then I came back to reality, I didn't feel scared, maybe a little excited, but that's all. It is funny when the adrenalin is flowing your life doesn't come past your mind, and the thought of dying wasn't there now. I didn't spend any time thinking of things I did, or things I didn't do, or things I would miss in the future if this was to be my last day, these things had already occurred to me earlier in the flight.

The flight up the coast seemed to take forever, but we finally reached the point of no return. It was late in the evening by now and as we turned into China, the lights of the city could be seen below. We were flying low so that their radar could not pick us up. Where time had gone so slowly, now it seemed to fly so quickly. As the MIG base was dark; no planes rushed up to meet us as we took our pictures and turned our plane to the coast. They could still shoot us down until we were past the 25 mile limit, and who knew if they would stop there, so we were on pins and needles all the way back to Japan.

As soon as we landed, we were brought to the ready room and kept in quarantine until the film was developed.

A high ranking officer who I had never seen before came into the room and congratulated all of us. "The pictures came out perfect. We could count and distinguish every plane on the ground" he said. Then continuing he told us that because we flew into enemy territory in an unarmed plane, that this was the most dangerous mission since the Korean War. He then told us that he was personally putting us in for the Air Medal.

Back in Japan and safe in my bunk that night I slept relieved and soundly like a baby.

When I was discharged there was no mention of the Medal, so I asked the Veterans Administration to check it out. They came back to me with the information that no such flight had taken place. The Navy would never admit that they sent an unarmed radar plane with 23 men aboard into China.

There is the question, why send a slow flying radar plane into China? They couldn't send a photo jet in, because it would have to be daylight, and the plane would have to fly over the base. Remember there was no U 2 to do this flight in 1956.

They could send a smaller jet with radar, but the equipment was nowhere near the quality of what was on a VW -1 Super Constellation. Remember this was a one time mission it could never be repeated once the Chinese were aware of what happened so everything had to be the best available.

VW-1 could fly at night. Could stand off at great distance to get good pictures. They only had to go maybe 30 minutes into China, and had a good chance of leaving Chinese air space before the MIG's would catch up.

So the commanding officers believed that sending a VW-1 radar plane was at the time the best solution. Also a unarmed plane probably would start another war if the plane was captured. Also they could say the plane mistakenly took the wrong turn if they were questioned about the flight.

Squadron Party

CHAPTER 20
THE SQUADRON PARTY

The squadron was commended on the success of the flight we took over China, so the Squadron Commander decided to throw a party for the three crews that were in Japan with 23 crewmen and six ground crew per plane plus the command. There would be about 100 sailors and of course their dates, if they brought one.

The only place big enough was the Fuji in Sagami, unless they wanted to go to Yokahama, but then if you got a hundred drunken party goers that far from base, it could be a real mess. At least in Sagami, we could all walk home – either to the base or a bar.

Everyone was there, and of course I brought Acami to show her off to the troops. She was dressed as only Acami could dress and you would not think she was Japanese the way she presented her self. She was always immaculate in western clothes, immaculate, but not over dressed, a thing of beauty. She could have been a model in Hollywood , and I was extremely proud to be with her on this night.

All the food and drinks were on the squadron. They had a full dance band and between sets, out came the strippers imported from Yokahama. I brought my camera and was taking plenty of pictures. I got a award winning shot of one of the dancers, and have included it in this book.

A great time was had by all, but then some pushing and shoving started on the dance floor.

I'm not sure how the fight started, but it was flight crew against the ground crew, and everyone was drinking and feeling their oats. There was always a bad feelings between the groups because the flight crew got extra flight pay and that seemed to stick in their craw. I had the Navy send my $100 a month home to my mother who dutifully put it in the bank. I had over two thousand dollars sitting there by the time I got discharged and the first thing I did was buy a 1952 Mercury Monterey with part of it.

I didn't get into the fight, I was protecting Acami and my camera, but in the midst of the melee, I set down my camera on a table away from the fighting so it wouldn't get broken, and when I looked back for it, it had disappeared.

The fight didn't last long and the Commander broke up the melee and closed the bar. It's too bad because I doubt if the squadron will ever do this again.

I went back to the Oasis and stayed the night. The next morning I was wondering about my camera so I kissed Acami goodbye and went over to the Fuji. There lying on the table was my camera. I was relieved.

On the base we did all our own developing at the Hobby Shop. So I went over and developed the film. Besides the pictures I had taken was a nude photo of a Josan. I had no idea who took the picture, but later someone recognized the bed spread as belonging to the Fuji Bar. I made a bunch of copies of the picture and gave them to all my squadron friends. The picture ended up taped inside everyone's lockers.

It was said that if you didn't want to go to town all one had to do was open their locker, and there was the inspiration to go into town.

CHAPTER 21
A TRIP TO THE
PHILIPPINES

One day early in April, 1956, the word came down; pack a bag for a few days as we are going to the Philippines. One of our pilots had a girlfriend in the Navy stationed in Manila, so a training flight for the plane crew, not including our Radar passengers was scheduled. So off we went down to Sangley Point. This was a Naval Air Station across the bay from Manila.

The first thing we noticed upon landing was the heat and humidity, it was stifling, something we were not used to being in cool Japan.

We were assigned to a mostly screened in hut. Our home away from home had chameleons running around the ceiling, and they would change color as they ran from one area to another. At least this was something we could watch when things got boring. We had no orders just have fun!

The city just outside the main gate was Cavite City and four of us decided to pay it a visit on our first evening. As we left the base, there were many jeepnees lined up (these were old jeeps left over from the Second World War) they were all painted up with a fancy fringe top. We climbed in one of them and asked the driver to take us to a good bar. The bar had strippers, we ordered rum and coke and left after one drink. We decided to see more of the town and the same driver was there waiting to take us to another placer, but this time he had a friend tagging along. We thought nothing of the additional man hanging on the side and to another bar we went. Again it was rum and coke as this seemed to be the national drink.

Then to another bar, the same taxi was waiting with a second friend tagging along. It must have been a slow night with no other business we thought, besides the Philippinos seemed so friendly probably because Macarthur saved them from the Japanese.

Many years later I became friends with a fellow architect who was from the Philippines. He didn't believe me when I told him of my experiences in his country, "We love the Americans," he replied.

After the third bar, there was another friend along. What a sight it must have been, a Jeepnee with 5 people inside and 3 hanging on the outside. In the next bar the rum and cokes got to me and I passed out. My crew mates took my watch and wallet for safe keeping and took me out to the taxi to sleep it off. I don't remember much more until we were heading back to the base, now with four of his friends hanging on. The jeep stopped about a hundred yards from the main gate. One of our crew jumped out, offered to pay the driver when he pulled out a gun. While he turned the gun on the rest of us, the first shipmate ran screaming toward the main gate and the Marine guards came running. By that time we were all out of the Jeep and the bad guys took off. The guards told us we were lucky and that just about every night they find a sailor staggering toward the gate with his guts hanging out. They said we were lucky we didn't lose our lives, I thought why didn't anyone warn us how dangerous Caviete City was. We decided that the next day we would go into Manila and see what the big city was all about and of course find out more information on what to do and what not to do.

Sunken Japanese Ship

We were told that there was a bus around the bay, but servicemen were now allowed to take it. "Too dangerous" we were told. "There are roving gangs in the countryside called hucks, they would stop buses and rob the passengers and a serviceman could get killed.

The only way to get to Manila was by Navy launches that went back and forth across the bay. Also we were told to travel in a group the larger the better. Keep your wallet in your front pocket, don't take more money with you that you feel you need. Keep two hands on your camera and don't eat or drink in the local establishments. For food and entertainment there was a large hotel in the center of the city and we were strongly advised to go there. And after our experience in Cavite, we believed everything we were told. So the next day six of the crew joined other passengers aboard a Navy launch for the 20 mile trip across the bay.

I was amazed as our launch wandered its way across the bay. It was a longer trip that I initially thought because we had to wander our way around and between rusting sunken Japanese ships sunk from the Second World War. I think half of the Japanese Navy was resting there. The water must not have been that deep because it seemed most of the ships were showing above the water. "Look at that," I said, "I bet that was a destroyer and that one over there was a battleship" I continued.

I wondered how many of their dead were entombed below in these ships - just like the Arizona in Hawaii.

In later years, the Japanese came and removed all the ships, collected the dead and hauled all the steel back to Japan where I bet if you bought a Toyota or Honda, some of that steel was in it.

We wandered around Manila for a few hours. I was amazed at how much destruction was still around ten years after the war. I took some great pictures of a bombed out cathedral where there were young children playing among the ruins.

We were hustled by beggars and shoved around by the crowds on the street, but I had my hands firmly grabbing my camera.

We finally made our way to the hotel that was suggested we should go to. It was great to get out of the sweltering heat and into air conditioning. The place was beautiful and we were told that it served as the headquarters for both the Japanese and the Americans later. I thought jokingly, "Macarthur slept here."

There was a beautiful bar that looked like a jungle with tigers painted on the walls. We ingested a cool beer, watched some exotic dancers perform and then decided to head back to the base. The launch didn't travel at night because of the sunken ships. It was getting late in the afternoon and we felt it was too expensive to stay the night at the hotel.

The next day we hung around the hut watching the lizards on the ceiling. I wondered where our pilots were that were supposed to take us back to Japan, and besides, I missed Acami.

Three days later, the pilots finally showed up. We were all filthy as no one brought enough clothes and supplies and with the heat we sweltered through our things pretty fast. We were all kind of broke by then too.

I don't remember the flight back, but I knew I never wanted to see the Philippines again. Our trip turned out to be a disaster the low light of my time in the Navy.

CHAPTER 22
CHERRY BLOSSOM TIME

When I got back from the Philippines, the first thing I did was go to see Acami. I had given Momasan money for three days, not knowing our pilot would not show up, so she put her to work. I asked her why she didn't wait for me to get back and that I would have made up the difference when I got back. "What happen you never come back, you be here long time you leave soon navy," she said. I tried to reason with her, but I knew in my heart that I would be leaving in a few weeks to go back to Hawaii and haven't told Momasan or Acami. I guess I just dreaded the day I would have to leave and pushed the thought out of my mind. I lied to Momasan and said "Never hatchi, I no go for long time." That seemed to calm her down and I stayed the night.

Spring was in the air and all the trees and plants were leafing out. I noticed that a row of cherry trees on the base just across the street from the Shinto Temple were in bloom.

I decided that I would like to go and take pictures of cherry trees and I thought what better place to see them then in Tokyo and around the Imperial Palace. I had never been to Tokyo so I asked squadron friends to come along, but I couldn't find anyone to come with. I was a little leery about going alone because it was such a big city and I didn't know my way around, but none of my friends had been there either and Acami would be no help as she hadn't been there either.

So the next morning bright and early, off to Tokyo I went. It's kind of funny looking back fifty years I did so many things that today would be considered dangerous. I hitch hiked from California to Minnesota and back again six times. I also would hitch hike from Dago to LA alone hundreds of times and traveled around Hawaii and Japan alone and never worried about my safety between the years of 18 and 21. I guess I was young and innocent to the trouble I could get into. I could write a book on just my adventures while hitch hiking.

One time in North Plat, Nabraska, I had my thumb out when a car pulled up. He hollered to me,

"Can you drive?" I said "yes." He threw the car keys at me and said ,"Get me to Omaha," as he passed out. I pushed him over to the passenger side , and drove him to Omaha. When he came to he told me he had been parting all the night before, and I was his only solution.

Another time I was hitchhiking at two in the morning in Larami, Wyoming, when a police car pulled up. I wasn't surprised because the cops would often check on service men hitchhiking to make sure their papers were in order. The police man said ,"You will never get a ride this time of night, because of the mountain between here and Cheyenne. Smart drivers don't want to travel this two lane road at night." "Come with me and I will give you a place to sleep till morning," he said. At the police station all the cells were full, so they brought me into the court room, gave me some blankets and a pillow. I slept on the judges desk, and in the morning they dropped me off at the same corner, and I picked up a ride in a short time.

I took the train from Sagami to Tokyo as it was only about 25 miles, so it didn't take long to get there. So there I was at the Tokyo main train station. The easiest way to get around a strange place was to take a taxi. I told the driver I was planning to take pictures around the Imperial Palace and to take me there. He suggested that I go to Hiba Park which was close to the palace grounds and he said "velly beautiful."

Hiba Park

He was right about Hiba Park. It was as lush a place as one could see, with stone bridges and small Japanese pavilions, a river and a lake. I took one picture which I consider the best picture I ever took of two ladies with an umbrella, looking over the scenery, I've included this picture in this book. You see a lot of sun umbrellas in Japan because the sun bothers their eyes. They cannot close their eyes tightly and so you see the umbrellas. The park was great, but no cherry trees in sight.

I walked over to the palace. It was a large area about two miles square with a mote running around it. I could see the palace from one vantage point and there were numerous stone towers that made for picture taking, but alas no cherry trees.

I wandered across the street to the Imperial Hotel designed by Frank Lloyd Wright. It was designed on a floating slab so that when an earthquake came, the building would float. Seeing that my plan when I got discharged was to go to college and take up architecture, seeing this building was important to me. In the front of the main entrance was a beautiful lily pond. I wandered around the lobby and took many pictures.

Now it was time to head back to Sagami and Acami. The only cherry blossoms I saw all day were the trees on the base.

Last Date

CHAPTER 23
SAYING SAYONARA

Sayonara in Japanese means goodbye forever. It was getting close to leaving and I pondered on how to tell Acami. Do I just disappear, leave without saying a word? This would not be fair to her or me. I would have married her if she would have agreed and the government would have said yes. This was my dilemma.

I finally decided to take her out to the base for an evening of dining and dancing and at the close of the evening, say goodbye forever. I wouldn't stay the night, as that would be painful for both of us.

So the plan was in the works, but first there were a lot of last minute duties to attend to before we left Japan. The plane had to be readied, our gear had to be packed, monies had to be exchanged and the last thing was to turn in our liberty pass and chow hall pass.

I kept just enough yen for my last night and the plan was in motion. Everything worked as planned when I picked up Acami. She was dressed beautifully, not a hair out of place and she looked like a beautiful princess on her way to the ball. This would make it much harder to say goodbye later in the evening. The evening went well and we had a wonderful steak dinner and danced the night away. A steak in Japan is a treat to remember. They hobble the cattle so they cannot run and then gorge them with food before they slaughter them, I'm sure everyone has heard of Colby beef.

We headed back to the Oasis and I'm sure everyone expected me to stay but when I got a few feet from the door I stopped, I kissed her, I told her how much I loved her, and that how I would have married her in a moment if my government would have let me.

She said she understood. I told her that if the government changed its mind or after I got discharged, I could fly back to get her and that would be our hope for the future. I kissed her again and said "sayonara, but for a little while," and walked away crying.

That was the last time I saw her and I still have that moment in my mind and a tear in my eye as I write and relive that moment in time, fifty years ago.

It seemed like a fantastic dream, but it did happen and I wonder what has become of Acami she would be sixty-eight years old if she is still alive.

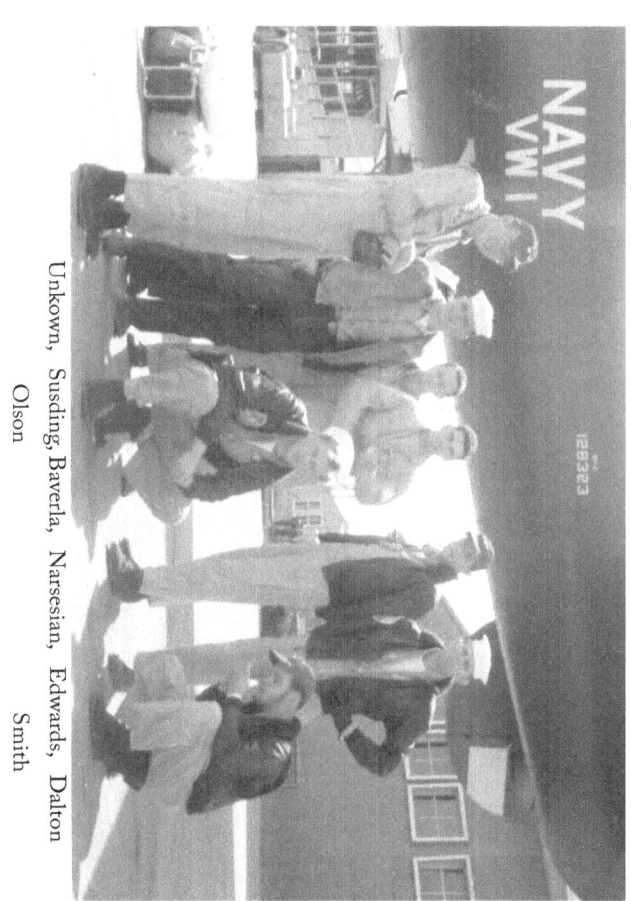

Unkown, Susding, Baverla, Narsesian, Edwards, Dalton

Olson Smith

Leaving for Hawaii

CHAPTER 24
LEAVING FOR HAWAII

It was the beginning of May 1956. My discharge date was June 9th, so I had very little time left in the service. Would I do it again? In a moment! My four years had been a wonderful time of growing up and seeing and experiencing other cultures. Join the Navy and see the world was the saying. My only regret was that I was never able to see Europe and the Mediterranean.

This would be my last flight in Nr4 and VW-1, the rest of my time would be spent mustering out. I looked forward to this last flight with the crew I had been with for so long. Little did I know that this trip to Hawaii would be so memorable.

Everything was set to go; liberty cards turned in, bags packed and goodbyes said. I thought back to my last goodbye with Acami. I had met and loved the most wonderful girl I thought I would ever meet again she was perfection in every way.

I looked out the window and watched the coastline of Japan disappear. Goodbye Fujisava, I said to myself, goodbye Acami, and with a tear in my eye I settled down for the long flight home where we would be in Hawaii before we left Japan because of crossing the International Date Line.

I wasn't working the radio and I was just sitting enjoying a cup of coffee when the flight engineer cut the power to one of our engines. We were more than two hours out or about 500 miles out at this time. "It was no problem," he said, we can still fly on three engines, but if we lose another engineer, we're in the drink."

"It was an oil leak" he stated, "so I shut the engine down before it froze out on us," so we are headed back to Japan. When we got near land, we started to dump fuel before landing to lighten the load and also to make it safe for landing on three engines. Besides, landing with a full load of fuel was dangerous if our landing wasn't quite right.

I took my camera and went back to one of the windows and took pictures of the gas pouring out of the wing tanks. "Get seated" came the order "we're going straight in." We landed and everyone was ordered to stay with the plane.

They pulled a ladder up to the troubled engine, and in about an hour, everything was fixed. It's a good thing we shut the engine down when he did. If the engine would have froze up all of a sudden, it could have been very dangerous, and we could have been swimming with the fishes.

But the oil leak was fixed and the engine sounded good and we were set to go again.

I said goodbye to Japan and Acami as the coast of Japan disappeared again from view. Everything seemed fine, we were in about the same place where our first engine problem happened. I was drinking another cup of coffee when déjà vu. There was a loud bang and the plane shook. I looked out the window and flames were shooting out of a different engine than our other problem. We were overloaded with all the fuel and supplies aboard and we would have definitely crashed if we had lost both engines while in the air.

I had my camera and got some good pictures of the flames shooting out of the engine, I was excited and didn't think of the problem we were in.

The engine was immediately shut down, fire bottles in the compartment put out the fire and it was time to dump fuel again and back to Atsugi as we headed for another three engine landing. We all looked at the smoking motor after landing; it was a mess and beyond repair.

Here we were; we had lost two different engines trying to fly to Hawaii and we're still alive. If our timing had been off and we had flew a little farther before all this happened, this book would never have been written.

I thought of all the times we had looked for downed planes and how we never found any. The only thing we could do now was to unpack our bags and return to the barracks until our problem was solved.

The engine was beyond repair and a new one would have to be sent out from Lockheed in Burbank, California, and that would take a couple of weeks before we were off again.

So here we were, no liberty card, low on money and stuck on base with nothing to do. I thought of Acami just a few miles away. Maybe I could borrow someone's liberty card, but then I thought this would be anticlimactic and too painful to go through again, It was better to leave everything as is. Here we are back in Japan and we might as well be on the moon.

My discharge date was looming just a month away. I could have raised hell and they would have sent me back on M.A.T.S. like last time. No way was I doing that again. This was my last flight with my old crew and come hell or high water, I was going back with my crew, besides the third time is the charm.

Now what to do while waiting a few weeks... I went over to the hobby shop and decided to build a model plane. I had built many stock models when I was a kid, but now I planned to build the best one I could. I picked out a two engine Navy pursuit bomber and went to work. In my youth the stick models I built used balsa strips, and the area between the balsa was covered with tissue paper. The paper was glued down, then wetted so it would stretch, and finely painted. On this model I made every surface out of balsa adding talcum powder in the surface paint and put many coats so the surface was smooth as glass. I then installed two gas engines. My former models a rubber band was used for power this was the first time I had used gas engines. With nothing to do but build this model and drink beer at the EM Club, I decided this was the best model ever built. I doubt that I would ever fly it; I would be afraid of crashing my work of art.

While building this model my mind went back to another time and another model that I was trying to make perfect, the best one I had ever built.

I was a young teenager and it was the summer of 1947. I was sitting at the dining room table putting the last peaces of orange tissue paper on the tail assembly. The rest of the completed model that was my pride and joy was sitting in the middle of the table safe from all harm that could come to it, or at least I thought.

The neighbor girl came by to play with my sisters. She came into the dining room and said,"Oh what a beautiful airplane," as she picked it up gingerly, and then in a split second crushed it together in her hands. I was startled and without thinking through the scissor I had in my hand at her. It bounced off her chest and you could see some sprinkles of blood forming on her dress. She screamed,"I am telling my daddy," and ran out of the house crying.

My mother came running into the room when she heard all of the commotion. She immediately ordered me to go over to her house and apologies to her parents and explain what had happened. This was no easy task because her father was the feared chief of police. I gingerly went over to her house, and apologiesed to her father, then I explained what had happened holding my crushed plane in my hands. He was understanding, but warned me to watch my temper. He said, I was lucky that the scissor bounced of her breast bone and left only two small punch wounds.

As I walked home I thought if that scissor was a few inches each way I could have caused sever damage. I don't know how something this bad could be lucky, but I guess this was my lucky day.

The engine finally had arrived, then it took time to install it and we were ready to take off again. I took the plane I built and attached it under the ECM desk because there were no electronic counter measures on a flight to Hawaii, so it would be safe there. So gear was stowed away, and we were ready to go again. Oh well, third time is the charm!

CHAPTER 25
A FLIGHT TO NOWHERE

I watched the coast of Japan pass under us for the third time and with some sadness I said Goodbye Japan, goodbye Acami and now the only view out of the window was the restless sea and I had to be in Treasure Island in a little over a week so I couldn't afford another problem. We passed the magic point where all the other problems happened so I guess we will make it this time.

As the miles flew by I kept thinking of Acami; what will happen to her?

Looking at Japan, nowadays Atsugi is still there but there is no Sagami. It is a place of the past that will never happen again. It took the Second World War and the Kamikaze pilots to create the place and it took the Korean War to make Atsugi an important base for the Navy. It took the ingenuity of the Japanese to make it a home away from home and I took the modernization of Japan to eliminate it from history. It was a one of a kind place that couldn't stand up to time and will never happen again.

I thought of all the times and crazy things that went on. One time some guys from a different squadron found a little Japanese guy and brought him around to all the bars. It was May Day and he was waving a little Russian Red Flag. They said "Look what we found…a communist." The guy seemed very happy as he waved his little flag, thinking back this incident gave me a chuckle and now it's back to Hawaii.

The distance to Barbers Point was over 3000 miles and it should be right below us, but all we could see was ocean. The pilot came over the intercom and told us we were lost. If we kept on flying we would finally run out of gas and a decision had to be made and fast.

What happened that had put us in this position no one knew. We could see nothing on the radar, no land in sight. We could pick up a homing beacon from Barbers Point, but that didn't tell us whether we were south of Hawaii or north of the islands. We could fly in one direction and the signal would get weaker which would tell us we were flying in the wrong direction. But we were low on gas and so our pilot had to make a decision, if he guessed wrong we would end up in the drink which could be the end of all of us!

I thought why didn't I go back on M.A.T.S., at least I would get there. The pilots must have determined that we were north of Hawaii. I'm not sure what went on in the cockpit, whether they triangulated with other radio signals, but as we flew south, islands started to appear on our radar. We were on our way and everyone was relieved. I don't remember being scared; excited yes, scared no.

We landed at Barbers Point with fumes left for gas. I'm sure we couldn't have flown more that a few more miles.

Later we found out what happened. The navigator had given a 2 degree heading the wrong direction which actually was a 4 degree error. And over three thousand miles, it had taken us a long way off in an area called No man's Land. It is the largest empty area of open ocean in the world. That's why when the Japanese attacked Pearl Harbor; they traveled through this area so they wouldn't be found out.

With being lost in this area and running low on fuel put us in deep trouble. You have to remember this was 50 years ago. Radar did no have a great range and there were no satellites for help and even radio was sometimes iffy.

Once while flying out of Barbers Point I tried to send a position report. I couldn't raise Hawaii, but my signal was picked up by a plane flying out of Florida and my position report was sent to Barbers Point by teletype. This is called bounce frequency, that's where a signal will bounce and come down thousands of miles away.

Well, everything turned out OK. We landed safely, I sold the model I made to a guy in the squadron and made it back to Treasure Island for my discharge in time.

It all started with the day we lost our world and ended when we found it, on a flight to nowhere.

The Crew
1955 NASAtsugi,Japan Crew#4

LtoR PrQnt Row: Gordon Olson (AT -3, Radio), Loren Siinding(A T -3, tIC), Fred Edwards (AT -3, Radar),Bill Smith (A -r- 2, Radar), Donel] !Lewis (ATC,Radar, ECC), Da]las H~)I~A T -2, Radio), Georg~ Lovens (AE-2, CIC), Anderson (Ltjg, CICO); Bradly (Ens., CIC), Dorsake (Ens., CIC), Marano (Ens., Navigator), Marciano (Ltjg., Co-pilot)

Lt~R S~cond Row: Paul Lindsey (AD-2, Crew Chief), Robert Nersesian (AT -2, Radar),George Murphy (AE'-I, I 'l Elec), Ken rIa/Is (AD-I, 151 FE (in tractor seat)); Albert Dalton (AL-I, 1'1 Radio), Robert Cloper (A T -J, Radio), Rooke (1I..t., PPC), \1ipke r~ns1GIC)t Ted Bauerla (AE-3, ELec), Caler Hall (AT -l,Radat), Allen Pettit (AD~I, FE (in cockpit door)

PROLOG

Our flight over China was definitely a flight to nowhere, because I just received a letter from the Department of the Navy. They have no record of the flight or of any medals to be awarded.

Due to the fact that there is no record of the flight. The only assumption to be made is that squadron officers were afraid of the repercussions if the flight came to light, and omitted all references of the mission, the plane, and the medal.

This is not a dream. I know it happened, because I was there and lived it fifty years ago.

PLANE NR-4 HISTORY

The history of NR. 4 is confusing because the Nose Number, and the Bureau number are different, and do not agree with Navy records.

I can only assume what might have happened. The first conclusion is that Bureau Numbers do not change, but nose numbers could change at any time.

Therefore my BR. NR. 128323 can be read on the plane in one of the pictures in this book so I know this is correct. The number was assigned to plane NR.-2 which was delivered to VW-1 in 1954 then six months later it was sent back to Lockheed for new equipment, was refurbished and I assume given a gray paint job and a new nose number NR-4. It was returned back to VW-1 in 1955 where our crew took it over thinking that it was a new plane.

The plane was transferred to NAMTC at Point Mugu, Ca. in 1958, was then transferred to NAF Litchfield Park AZ. For storage in 1959, and scraped in 1965.

Now for the confusion. The records show a different NR-4 with a bureau NR. of 131390. It was delivered to VW-1 in Oct. 1954, and transferred to VW-2 on 22, May 1956.This is almost impossible because we didn't get back from Japan till about that time, and I don't remember my plane being shipped out probably a day after we arrived. This NR-4 crashed in Germany on 22, May 1962 with the loss of all hands aboard.

So which plane is the right NR-4? Who knows?

HISTORY OF VW-1

Airborne Early Warning Squadron One evolved from a VC-11 detachment, and was commissioned on 18, Jan. 1952 at Barbers Point, Hawaii.

There first plans were delivered in1953 they were PB-1W's the Navy version of the B 17 Flying Fortress. In Oct. 1954 the squadron received there first EC121K Warning Star which is the radar version of the Super Constellation.

A permanent detachment was established in WESPAC to provide the Seventh Fleet with AEW coverage at Barbers Point, with Detachment Able in NAS Atsugi, Japan, and Detachment Baker in the USAF base in Naha, Okinawa.

In 1957 VW-1 moved to NAS Agena, Guam, and was given the mission of weather reconnaissance.

This was a change in mission because aerial surveillance had changed with the changing times. Meteorological crew training, and special equipment was installed in the planes to make it effective for airborne weather observation and reporting.

The Squadron was disestablished in 1971 at that time the men and airplanes were absorbed into VQ-1

Places And Date

Joined the Navy   June 9, 1952

Boot Camp Great Lakes, Ill.   June 9, 1952 to Sept.1, 1952

Airman Prep School, Norman, Ok.   Sept. 15, 1952 to Nov. 15, 1952

Electronic School, Memphis, Ten.   Nov. 15, 1952 to June 1, 1953

NAS North Island San Diego, Ca. Base Communication   July 1 to July 1, 1954

NAS Barbers Point, Hawaii Base Radio,   Aug. 14, 1954 to Nov. 14, 1954

VW-1 Barbers Point, Hawaii,   Nov. 14, 1954 to June 1, 1956

First trip to Japan   June 1, 1955 to Aug. 1, 1955

NAS Barbers Point, Hawaii,   Aug. 1; 1955 to Feb. 1, 1956

Escape and Evasion School,   Aug. 1955

Radio School NAS North Isl. And home on leave Oct. Nov. 1955

Second trip To Japan,   Feb. 1, 1956 to May 20, 1956

Iwo Jima for three days   Feb. 1956

Flight over China,   Mar. 1956

Philippines for six days   Apr.1956

Back to Barbers Point, Hawaii   May 1, 1956

Engine repaired then back to Hawaii,   May 20, 1956

Leave for Treasure Island Ca.   June 1, 1956

Discharged   June 9, 1956

GLOSSARY

A partial list of words some are Japanese and some are English.

Arigato----Thank You

A so desuka----Is that so?   I understand.

Butterfly----To jump from one romance to another.

Chichi----Jane Russell had them, Dolly Parton has them.

Choto matte----Just a minute

Dia jobu----Okay.

Dame----No good, lousy.

Domo arigato----Thank you very much.

Gohan----Boiled rice, or food.

Gomen nasai----I beg your pardon.

Ichi ban----The best, number one.

Konnichi wa----Good afternoon

Kudasai----Give me.

Mamasan----Lady of the house.

Never hatchee----Sailor English, meaning never happen.

Nobody home upstairs----English, meaning dumb or no brains.

Ohayo gazimasu----Good morning, often just Ohio.

Okane----Money, and you would need it.

Presento----Sailor English meaning a gift.

Sayonara----Good bye, or good night.

Takusan----Many, or a large amount.

AIR MEDAL

The Air Medal was established by President Franklin D. Roosevelt on May 11, 1942 and made retroactive to 1939.

The Air Medal is awarded to any person while serving with the Armed Forces of the United States who has distinguished themselves by meritorious achievement while participating in aerial flight.

Awards may be made to recognize single Acts of Merit or Heroism or for meritorious service. Awards of the Air Medal is primarily intended to recognize those personnel who are on current crew member flying status which requires them to participate in aerial flight, performing a noteworthy act in the performance of their duties.

.